ACTIVATE YOUR GREATNESS

ACTIVATE YOUR GREATNESS

ALEX TOUSSAINT

HENRY HOLT AND COMPANY

NEW YORK

Henry Holt and Company
Publishers since 1866
120 Broadway
New York, New York 10271
www.henryholt.com

Henry Holt® and Ⓗ® are registered trademarks of Macmillan Publishing
Group, LLC.

Library of Congress Cataloging-in-Publication Data

Names: Toussaint, Alex, author.
Title: Activate your greatness / Alex Toussaint.
Description: First edition. | New York : Henry Holt and Company, 2023.
Identifiers: LCCN 2023017112 (print) | LCCN 2023017113 (ebook) |
    ISBN 9781250852038 (hardcover) | ISBN 9781250852021 (ebook)
Subjects: LCSH: Conduct of life. | Success. | Achievement motivation.
Classification: LCC BJ1589 .T68 2023 (print) | LCC BJ1589 (ebook) |
    DDC 131—dc23/eng/20230626
LC record available at https://lccn.loc.gov/2023017112
LC ebook record available at https://lccn.loc.gov/2023017113

Our books may be purchased in bulk for promotional, educational, or business use. Please contact your local bookseller or the Macmillan Corporate
and Premium Sales Department at (800) 221-7945, extension 5442, or by
e-mail at MacmillanSpecialMarkets@macmillan.com.

First Edition 2023

Designed by Omar Chapa

Printed in the United States of America

1   3   5   7   9   10   8   6   4   2

This book is dedicated to all the people who believed in me, and who gave me opportunities, delivered inspiration, and provided me with light in the darkest times.

This book is also dedicated to anyone out there who is struggling and having trouble believing in themselves, but is finding a way to keep pushing.

CONTENTS

CONTENTS

ACTIVATE YOUR
GREATNESS

INTRODUCTION

It's one in the afternoon. 1300 hours. My parents have just dropped me off at a military school in the middle of Nowhere, Missouri, some 1,200 miles from my home on Long Island. I'm twelve years old, a sixth grader. I swear I saw a smirk on my dad's face as my parents said goodbye, walked away, and left me.

I'm in the Admissions Office. The guy with me now, a major, is wearing a stiff-looking black uniform jacket. He had been extremely polite and attentive with my parents, like he was the nicest guy in the world. But the moment they were out of sight, his smile vacated his face. He tells me not to worry, that he'll take care of me, but his words lack any conviction. He beckons me outside, walking me into the bright sunshine onto what he tells me is the "quad." It's a giant square slab of concrete, about half the size of a football field, right in the middle of the campus, and is surrounded by the barracks, the mess hall, some classroom buildings, and the Admissions Office.

I'd spend a lot of time on the quad in the next three years. Every morning all of the cadets in the school were required to report here for roll call and to raise and salute the American flag. Every evening, we met here again, to lower it. And the entire school was required to meet here in the mornings, afternoons, and evenings to do our exercises—the marching and the drills—every single day, no matter the weather. Monsoon-like rain. Sleet. Snow. We'd do our drills when it was minus 10 degrees and you couldn't feel your fingers and couldn't move your toes. On midsummer afternoons, we marched for hours in heavy trench coats under the blazing 110-degree sun. We also had to stand at attention. Four hours straight of not moving at all. I learned not to lock my knees. If you did, you'd fall out, face-first onto the concrete. Happened all the time.

Any bad behavior in school meant even more time on the quad, doing extra marches and drills, and standing at attention. It's the place I remember most about my time at military school. A little taste of hell on earth.

But I didn't know any of this at the time. Now, I'm just standing in the middle of the quad watching the major—the same guy who just told me that he'd take care of me—walk back to the Admissions Office, his shiny black shoes clacking on the hot concrete.

I'm all alone. I'm small for my age. I'm wearing cargo shorts and a red T-shirt and my big, black, thick-rimmed glasses. I looked like a nerd-ass motherfucker. My bags are on the concrete behind me. I stare at the mess hall. The campus is eerily still and quiet. I want to sit down, but I'm petrified. Literally. I don't feel like I can move. I stand there for five minutes, then ten minutes, not knowing what the hell I am supposed to be doing.

Suddenly, from somewhere on the periphery, I hear a huge, roaring noise. A cacophony of voices, screaming and cussing. A surge of adrenaline rushes through my body. Fight or flight.

And then I see them—a small group of people who I would later learn was a mix of cadets, drill sergeants, and officers. Eight of them in total. They've sprung out from behind some bushes and are now sprinting toward me. They'd been hiding, watching me and waiting. As they rush me, I recoil and put my hands up in front of my face.

Then they're in my face, yelling all at once. The spray from their spit smears my glasses.

"Get the fuck down, you piece of shit! Get the fuck down on the ground!" one of them screams at me, mere inches from my ear.

I start to go down, slowly, still in shock, my mind and body unable to move in concert.

"No, you little shit! Not like that! Get the fuck up!" the same guy yells at me. He's the one who seems to be in charge. He turns to another guy and points to the ground.

"Cadet, show this little shit how it's done!"

The cadet drops straight to the concrete and does ten quick, powerful push-ups, and then springs back up, his back ramrod straight.

The man in charge turns to me. "Now, you. Get the fuck down and do it right!"

This time, I drop. I do push-ups until he tells me to stop. Then the man orders me to roll over onto my back. I do flutter kicks, pointing my legs out in front of me and scissoring them in the air. My stomach burns. If—no, *when*—one of my feet touches the ground, I'm forced to start all over again.

I do this for fifteen minutes straight—push-ups alternating with flutter kicks—with all eight of the guys watching me, yelling at me and reveling in my ineptitude, my pain, and my fear.

What I'm doing now, I'll learn later, is called "getting smoked." It's used as punishment for bad behavior. I would get smoked a lot in the next few years.

• • •

I hated my dad at that moment. Hated him more than anyone or anything I had ever hated in my life. It felt reciprocal. *He sent me* here? *It's not just that he doesn't love me, he must hate me. Damn that asshole.*

Later in life, I'd come to understand why he did what he did. Or at least, I'd see his rationale. Up to this point, I'd been a total disaster. I'd been kicked out of every school I'd been enrolled in. I'm talking preschool, elementary, middle. I had no respect for my teachers or, really, for any authority figures. I had no respect for myself. Though I'd somehow managed to avoid serious misconduct, some of the people I hung out with were starting to run into real trouble with the law. I was not exactly on the pathway to success. My dad would explain later that he was just buying me time, trying to keep me from getting into real trouble, with the law or worse. He wanted to give me a chance to get my head on straight.

But still . . . *What the fuck was this?* I didn't know places like this even existed. I was the youngest person at the military school, not even close to being mentally, emotionally, or physically mature enough to handle it. At the time, it only fucked me up worse. It made me feel less loved by my parents. It destroyed any confidence—and thus, love—I had for myself. I already had a toxic relationship with my dad at that point, my hatred for him simmering within me. Sending me to military school just made it all bubble and then erupt to the surface. It crushed me. It still hurts to this day if I really stop and think about it.

But I would eventually learn a way to use that pain. I would own it. And if you want, you, too, will be able to use your pain as inspiration.

. . .

That first night at military school, I cried myself to sleep. My roommate didn't say a word to me or even so much as look at me for the first couple of days. He'd been at the school for a semester already. I guess he knew that it was best that I get this part over with, that there was nothing anyone could say or do to make it any better. The crying was only the last gasp of denial of a life left behind—and a realization that the life yet to come was only going to get worse.

The school's student body was comprised of kids from all over the place—West Coast, East Coast, the South, the Midwest, and even Alaska. Some were rich kids who had tested their parents' patience and failed. There were dirt-poor kids who seemed grateful just to have three real meals a day and a bed and a roof over their heads. There were kids who were racist as hell and didn't even try to hide it. There were plenty of kids who already had records for some really bad shit—theft, battery, selling drugs.

And here we were, all thrown in together, a forced assimilation. There was no privacy. In the barracks, we had to keep our doors open at all times. There were no doors on the bathroom stalls. We all showered together in a square room, with twelve showerheads. The showerheads alternated cold and hot: One sprayed water so frigid that you couldn't stand under it for more than five seconds. The next was so scalding hot that it blistered your skin if you stayed under it for too long. We walked through them all, in a row, as if on a conveyor belt. A drill sergeant barked out instructions, keeping us moving, ten seconds per showerhead. He grinned as he watched us, exhilarated by our displays of pain.

I remember standing outside of that shower room on that first day, buck naked, with eleven other kids, holding my little shower caddy and thinking, *Man, this was not in the brochure.*

I made my bed with hospital corners, the sheets as tight as I could get them. A drill sergeant came by every morning and smacked my bed with his saber. If that saber didn't bounce, I'd get demerits, or "sticks," as they were known. In my closet, my uniform had to be perfectly hung, with the sleeves pinned behind it. I wiped down my room and closet every day. My success, or lack of success, in doing this task was tested daily by a drill sergeant, who donned a white glove and ran a finger on the tops of all surfaces and in the corners of the room. Anything that soiled those white gloves in the slightest meant more sticks.

At meals, we had to sit on the edge of our chairs—so far on the edge that the bolts near the front of the seat had to be visible. Our backs had to be straight, at a perfect right angle. We ate in a squared motion—fork to food, raised straight up, then straight across to the mouth, a perfect upside-down L. Any deviation in form meant more sticks.

You couldn't look to your left or your right during mealtime. Only straight ahead. And if the dude sitting across from you made you laugh, or even smile, they'd take your food from you— your meal now over—and then they'd march you to the quad and smoke you. We couldn't have sugar—of any kind. No candy. No soft drinks. No dessert.

If I wanted someone to pass me the salt during a meal, or had a request for really anything, I had to use this exact phrase:

"Sir! High Speed Low Drag Foxtrot Company RAT Toussaint respectfully asking to speak."

"Speak," would come the response from a drill sergeant or officer.

"Sir! High Speed Low Drag Foxtrot Company RAT Toussaint respectfully asking to take up his tray."

"Take it."

That string of words still pops into my head sometimes. "High Speed Low Drag" meant that we had to do everything at a high pace, no dragging of our feet, no slow playing. It's military shorthand for doing anything and everything at *all* times at game speed and with excellence. "Foxtrot" was my company. And

"RAT" was what I felt like. It was also an acronym for what I was: a "Recruit at Training."

If you received ten or more sticks by the Thursday of each week, you had to march them off during the weekend. Unfortunately, I led the league in sticks. Each stick equaled one marching tour, and each tour was fifteen minutes long. Most weekends I was in military school, I was marching—I averaged between forty and sixty tours a weekend, more than you could humanly do. That meant I just marched—back and forth across the quad while holding my rifle—for, at times, seven or eight hours straight, with stops only for a meal. It's possible that I spent more hours marching on the quad than I spent doing anything else in my life at that time, aside from sleeping. If I talked to another cadet marching near me, it meant more tours. If I let my mind wander and wobbled from my lane, more tours. So how'd I get through it? I had to block everything out, concentrate on my breathing, concentrate on that next step I had to take, because the last thing I needed was more tours. It was the first time in my life that I knew I needed to change to endure. I was good at getting into trouble at military school, yes, but even I knew there were some limits I had to stick to.

The drill sergeants owned us. They barged into our rooms—for whatever reason they saw fit, anytime, day or night—and made us do drills or smoked us. They took special pleasure in doing this during "rec" time—the only tiny, daily piece of respite we had, where we could just nap or chill or do nothing. They told us when we could eat, sometimes making us sit at the mess hall table with our food tantalizingly right in front of us, which we were not allowed to touch until they said so. It wasn't even good food, but we were often starving. There was no entertainment either, no radios or TVs.

It was a prison without the bars. Trying to run away was useless. The school was in the middle of nowhere. You hear stories about actual inmates getting tattoos. We didn't do that, but one night, a few of my fellow cadets and I pierced our ears with semi-sterilized paper clips. We'd put in our earrings when no "people of authority" were around, the one act of rebellion we did that came without the consequence of sticks and more marching.

I couldn't call my parents for the first eight months I was away at school. So I'd write them letters. I addressed them all to my dad. I told him to fuck off and that I hated him. I knew my mom would read the letters, and I dared her to do so. I wanted to hurt her, as well, for allowing my dad to send me to this hellish place and not intervening to get me out of it. The first time I was able to call home, my mom answered. My dad never got on the phone. It wasn't hard for me to picture him sitting in his big chair in the living room, listening and grinning from ear to ear.

I had failed at everything I had ever done in my life to that point. I felt like a total loser at age twelve. I was depressed, anxious, insecure, and angry. Military school only served to heighten those feelings.

I didn't know it at the time, but I had another decade of disaster ahead of me. Military school was only halftime—a long, dark three-plus years that would only fuel the fires of my future failures. . . .

• • •

I know what you might be thinking right now: *Whoa, you're starting off a book that's supposed to be motivating me with some dark-ass shit.*

You're damn right I am.

Failure and feeling stuck in darkness are universal. I don't care if you're a grocery bagger, an NBA star, or a CEO. You have failed at something. And you will again. You have been in a dark place, felt down, felt like a loser, felt out of place. And you will again.

But all of that failure, that pain, that darkness, is useful if we make it so. It can become our superpower. I want to tell you the story of how I made it become mine.

• • •

I am a Peloton instructor. The bike I ride for a living is stationary. But it can take us anywhere we want to go.

I teach classes to hundreds of thousands of people from all over the world, people of all races, nationalities, ages, genders, religions, income levels, political affiliations. The classes are motivational, intended to change us all physically for the better. More important than that, though, they are intended to change us all mentally for the better.

I ride the bike that appears on screens in people's homes, garages, attics, gyms, living rooms. I choose the route we will take, when and how far we will climb, how hard or how easy we'll go along the way. I choose the cadence and the resistance we put on the bike. I choose both the soundtrack to the ride, and what I will say to keep my riders going, to push us, and to get us to the finish line.

But I do not ride ahead of my riders. I do not ride behind them, either. I ride right beside them, *with* them. On the bike, we are all one.

I am blessed to do what I do. It is a privilege to motivate, to give people a piece of myself and try to help them. I never, ever forget that. I prepare intensively for every class I teach. I give it everything I have when I'm on the bike. Even when I'm feeling off or sick, I find a way to overcome it.

I do this for us because I know what it's like on the other side. I know what it's like to be depressed, to doubt yourself, to fail and let negativity take complete control of your life.

And I know what it's like to overcome it all. And with this book, I aim to help you—help *us*—do the same thing as we ride alongside each other and inspire each other to greatness.

My very first experience with a stationary bike came a decade ago. I had on a pair of sweaty yellow rubber gloves. With a rag in one hand and a bottle of disinfectant reeking of ammonia in the other, I cleaned that bike, cleaned the hell out of it. Sprayed the handlebars and the seat and the water bottle holder and the neck and the pedals. Wiped it all down. And then moved on to the next one. There were fifty of them in total.

I also scrubbed toilets, wiped counters, cleaned windows, and dusted sills. I took out the trash. I mopped the floors. I did all of the so-called dirty work as a janitor at a spin class studio in East Hampton, New York.

It was a job that completely changed my life.

This book is about that change, that journey, the dark path that I traveled until I got that job, and the light that came out of it that has continued to lead me. It's about the steps I took—to feel good, look good, and do better—that finally allowed me to activate my greatness.

This book is about how you can do it, too. It's about how we'll do it together. We all have greatness within us. When we look in the mirror every morning, we are looking at the Chosen One. In the words of the great Alice Walker, "We are the ones we've been waiting for."

But we all have things that get in the way of our greatness—a lack of confidence, a toxic relationship, an unhealthy mindset. In other words, the negativity in our lives—a rather formidable opponent. This is what we must overcome.

We start at the bottom of a mountain. The climb up the mountain is the way we will overcome the negativity. The mountaintop is where we activate our greatness.

Here are the steps:

- **FEEL GOOD**
- **LOOK GOOD**
- **DO BETTER**

The first step up that mountain is to feel good. Feeling good is about believing in ourselves, in our own worth and greatness.

The next step is looking good. But this isn't about our hair, our clothes, or the shape of our bodies. This is about the inside, that internal light that radiates out into the world because we feel good about ourselves. That *true* beauty that's impossible to ignore or deny, to any observer and even to ourselves.

These first two steps are all about us. They're about concentrating on ourselves and ourselves alone. That may sound selfish, but it's a good kind of selfish, because we must love, help, serve, and believe in ourselves before we can do anything else. Once we've made those first two steps toward greatness, we can move on to the third step: Do better.

To do better is the mountaintop. It's the point at which we've overcome the negativity. But unlike the first two steps, this one is not all about us. It isn't about losing weight or hitting a personal record or making more money or driving an expensive car. It isn't about the self. In fact, it's about the sublimation of the self. Because we didn't grind all the way to the top just so everyone else could see us. It's the other way around. We got to the mountaintop so that *we can see everyone else.*

Doing better is about others, about reaching out and helping them, about spreading the strength and confidence—the love, really—that we have created for ourselves. But it's also about us. When we do better, we create a rising tide, whether in our families or our communities. As that tide lifts everyone else up, it lifts us up, too.

But this isn't our endpoint. Nope. Because when we reach that summit, the next thing we will do is to start back down, covering all of that ground we worked so hard to gain. We will look around us—to our families, friends, coworkers, communities, strangers—and extend our hands out to anyone and everyone who needs our help taking those steps to join us on the mountaintop. We will win *together*.

That's what activating our greatness is.

. . .

Like the bike, this book is also "stationary." It's just words on paper or a screen, or words coming to you through some earbuds. By definition, it goes nowhere. But, like the bike, it can take us anywhere.

The Peloton platform rewards us when we reach a new personal record, also known as "hitting a PR." In its most basic sense, that means going faster and harder and farther than we ever have before. In a deeper sense, though, it means reaching a personal record in our lives. Everything we do in a class—how we prepare, focus, reach and push ourselves to hit our PRs—is practice in preparation for real life. That's why we do it at game speed. High speed. Low drag.

Same with this book. We are going to demonstrate to ourselves and to the world that if we can do it here—if we can take inspiration from a stationary source and set it in motion in real life and real time—we can do it anywhere.

A personal record isn't really about making more money or losing weight or any of the other things that self-help books have been written about for a century. It's about us, about reaching the point where we can feel good about ourselves, look good, and do better by the world. This isn't a physical fitness book. It is a mental and spiritual fitness book. Being in good physical shape is extremely important in life, but nothing you do in life is worth a damn if you aren't also mentally and spiritually fit. My coaching is for your mind, to enable you to control and connect with your body.

I've lived through this. My story is not any more important than anyone else's, but I believe it can help us. It's fully me. It's open and vulnerable. It's authentic. I was once extremely depressed. Down-and-out. Broke and broken. I failed at everything I did in life and didn't learn a thing from those failures, and even thought that I was too late and too far gone to redeem myself. I was an extremely negative person who suppressed all of those negative emotions, which made me even more miserable.

And then, after hitting rock bottom with my dad and in my life, I took a deep stare in the mirror and started up the mountain. It didn't happen in one day. It was gradual. But it happened. I saw the mountain. I stood at the bottom. I didn't know exactly how to climb it, but I made the decision that I would start up it anyway, that I would put myself out there and try. And then, I took a step.

My journey wasn't easy. There were advances and retreats, certainly not a straight line to the top. It never has been and it never will be. Yours won't be, either. The route is uniquely yours. But it *will* move upward if you make the commitment to yourself.

My journey is also far from over. It's a work in progress. In fact, in some ways, it has only just begun. I start at the bottom of a mountain every single day and make the climb.

If I can make this journey, we all can.

· · ·

I am honored and filled with gratitude that you have chosen to come along on this journey with me. Thank you from the bottom of my heart.

This book is about us. We're going to do this together. I am headed back down the mountain with my arms extended, toward you. Reach out and grab them.

PART ONE

FEEL GOOD

CHAPTER 1

PREPARING TO FAIL

Let's talk a little bit about what "feeling good" means. It's the first fundamental step we must take in order to push away negativity and activate our greatness. It's how we feel about ourselves when we climb into bed every night, and how we feel about ourselves when we wake up in the morning. If we don't feel good, there is no way to make the most of the twenty-four hours that we've been blessed with every day. Instead, we bullshit our way through those twenty-four hours. And bullshitting can become a habit, and our daily habits become our lives.

Feeling good is a mindset. It boils down to this simple phrase, which was drilled into me by my coworker Christine D'Ercole when I joined Peloton: *I am, I can, I will, I do*. Feeling good requires discipline. It requires execution, repetition, and focus. It requires confidence, a confidence that comes from the inside and not from "likes" on Instagram and Facebook.

I have to admit it's a little strange for me to read what I've written here so far. I'm able to write this book now in an authentic way because I've lived it. But there was a long time in my life—a very long time—when if someone had told me I would ever say these words and really mean them, I would have laughed in their face. Back then, I never, ever thought I'd be in a position to help and motivate others, because I couldn't even help or motivate myself.

One of the cornerstones of feeling good is finding our gratitude. I find mine every morning. I give thanks that I woke up. I think about my family, friends, and dogs, and how blessed I am to be able to give people a piece of my life, a piece of me, every day. I am eternally grateful that there are people out in the world who want to listen to what I have to say because for a long time in my life, I felt that no one cared at all.

• • •

My parents are both first-generation immigrants from Haiti. My dad was born in Cap-Haïtien. In 1967, he came to the United States at age ten and moved to Queens. My mom was born and raised in Port-au-Prince and came to the United States in 1981, when she was twenty-one, to study. Shortly after she arrived, the two of them met and were married. Neither of them spoke English when they arrived in America, only French and Creole, and neither of them had much money. But the United States was the land of promise to them, and they both sought out the opportunity to improve their lives and live to their fullest potential. They strived to give their children a better start in life than they had—the American Dream. Failure was not an option for either of them.

My parents had three children. I am the youngest by quite a bit, born nine years after my oldest brother, Martial, and six years after my middle brother, Phil.

My mom, Judith, was in education all of her life, as a school-teacher and an administrator. She believed that a person should be as educated as possible, that doing so freed your mind and opened up a world of opportunities. Her goal when she came to the United States was to earn a PhD, and she went after it, full throttle. Along the way, she collected various degrees—a BA in secondary education, a master's in linguistics. When she got that PhD, it was in education. She taught herself how to speak English, and then taught English as a second language to other nonnative speakers, and also taught one of her native tongues, French. By the end of her long professional career, which included stops in Queens and the Hamptons, she was running the language department for a large school district in New York.

My mom is a virtuous woman who has an incredible work ethic. She was ultracaring but strict with all her kids. "Tough love" was her mantra. She made it crystal clear that we were to get a good education and that we all had to apply ourselves to what-ever we did in life. Her own path embodied that plan. My mom always had to be the best at whatever she did, though she would never have said it like that. But deep down, it was true. She had to have the best education. She spoke all of her languages with impeccable grammar. She was determined to be the best teacher in the school and the best administrator in the district.

She was always put together (and still is, to this day) and never left the house without her hair and nails done and wearing a nice outfit. I used to ask her why she cared what she looked like when she walked out to the driveway to get the mail, and why she cared if I wore a du-rag or a hoodie when I left the house. And she would tell me that, well, she just chose to do it that way, that in always making herself presentable, she was making sure that she was always prepared and ready for any opportunity. "You never know when something might present itself," she would tell me. I think it was also her way of validating all of the work she had put in to get to her station in life, and all of the sacrifices she made for our family. And I think that the way she carried herself and her desire to be the best she could be was also a way of assimilating into her new country and its culture, though she never shared this with me. I would only come to understand, much later, that it was also some sort of suit of armor, a way of protecting herself and her family.

I learned from her by example, though many of those lessons would take a while to seep into me. I witnessed her working her ass off. She always outworked her job and her job title. If she was teaching French, she worked like she ran the entire language department. If she ran the language department, she worked like she ran the school. And so forth. She always had that mindset. Nothing was given to her along the way. She earned everything she got.

My mom always called me her miracle baby. When she started experiencing contractions and went to the hospital, the doctors discovered that I had stopped moving. So they induced her immediately. When I was delivered, my umbilical cord was wrapped around my neck. I survived by the grace of God.

She also used to call me her bodyguard. And I did feel protective of her (and still do). Whenever she went out to do errands or anything like that, I always begged to go with her. If she went to the grocery store, I'd tag along and push the cart. I'd even accompany her to the nail salon and just sit in a chair near her for hours. I don't know why I felt the need to protect her—she didn't need it, that's for sure. In retrospect, I realize that maybe it was *me* who wanted—and needed—that protection.

My dad's name, Martial—as in "warlike" or "martial arts"—suited him well. He is and always was a strict and tightly wound man, like a clenched fist. Serious. No bullshit. He, too, dressed up whenever he left the house. His Afro was always neatly trimmed, and he wore good-smelling cologne. His suit game was tight, all three-pieces. He never drank or smoked. The one activity he did for fun was ballroom dancing, and he was pretty good at it. But he didn't do it all that much. He was all about his work. A natural-born grinder. He loved to work, almost to the point of obsession. It was like he was always running, seeking to stay one step ahead of something that was trying to catch him. He couldn't stop. His work provided him with dignity. It made him proud. He was also stubborn as hell and a man of routine. He's stuck with the same barber nearly all his life, even when we moved two hours away from that barbershop.

Before he met my mom, my dad had enlisted in the navy. He was a machinist mate on a battleship and spent three and a half years at sea during the Vietnam War, though he never saw any direct action. He loved being in the military. The discipline side of it fit his personality very well—he's continued to take three-minute showers ever since. After he left the navy, he returned to Queens and began to work for a heating oil company, eventually grinding his way up to become a project manager. He designed and maintained oil tanks of all sizes, from the ones found in residential homes to the biggest commercial terminals. After my parents got married, they moved to Coram, a town near the midpoint of Long Island where they had some family around, and he commuted an hour or so into the city every day for work.

My dad had a few different sides to him. He was strict as hell—stricter than my mom—and was particularly harsh on my brothers. He made them do feats of endurance, like running ten miles. He forced them to take part in karate fights with him. He wanted his kids to be as tough as he was.

I was so young at the time that I didn't participate in the runs or the karate fights. Instead, my dad made me watch. And even though I was only observing, the message he was sending came across loud and clear. In fact, it was maybe even more effective because I *didn't* have to run or fight, which made me feel guilty. The message was: My dad required discipline in the household. And that was that.

But, back then, my dad was also a family- and community-minded man. He was our primary breadwinner and provided the household with structure, integrity, and a backbone. He often spent large portions of the weekends driving around town and checking in on family members—my uncles, aunts, and cousins—as well as family friends. He taught countless neighborhood kids how to drive and swim. A lot of people around town came to him for advice, like he was the Godfather of Coram.

During this period of my life, my dad and I were best friends. When I wasn't with my mom, I'd tag along with *him* wherever he went. We'd go to Home Depot on the weekends. I'd ride around with him when he checked in on people around the neighborhood. During these trips, he'd sometimes buy me some french fries from McDonald's, a true treat coming from him. I was the third kid, the youngest by a large margin, and though he was still very strict with me, he did, on occasion, spoil me in a way he hadn't spoiled my older brothers.

But in 1998, when I was six years old, everything in our family—and my relationship with my dad—changed dramatically.

• • •

That year, my dad was diagnosed with colon cancer. It was not caught early. He had to have his entire colon removed. I would learn much later that, at one point, the doctors told my mom that he was on his deathbed.

I didn't immediately know this information because it was impossible to get from him. It's not like he ever sat us down and told us what was happening. He was too proud to do that, and that's not what men of his generation, particularly those from the macho Haitian culture, did. And he wouldn't let my mom tell us, either.

My mom and brothers knew more than I did, of course, but they did a good job of shielding me from most of what was going on. At age six, I had no real grasp of what the word "cancer" meant. But I do remember that the household was tense at that time. I remember thinking that it was strange that he had a long stay in the hospital, made frequent trips to the doctor after he got out, spent days and weeks at home in bed, and no longer left the house to go to work. I remember thinking that something was really wrong and that it was something I did not understand at all. I was terrified, too, when I saw how all of this drastically changed my dad—physically, yes, but more important, mentally and emotionally.

The dynamic in my family was altered in an instant. My dad never worked again. My mom was thrust into the role of bread-winner, which meant that she had to work longer hours, teaching and going to school at the same time. She was away from home a lot.

My dad survived the cancer in body but not necessarily in mind. He now had to do the household chores and handle the cooking of the meals because of my mom's schedule. Over time, he gradually stopped paying attention to my older brothers, maybe believing that they had received enough years of his discipline to make them men. Instead, his attention shifted to me, the one kid who had not been put to the test. And it wasn't the type of attention I wanted or needed.

Suddenly, I was in trouble with him all of the time. My brothers stayed out of it, and my mom wasn't around to deflect it. It created a feedback loop, a vicious cycle. I'd get in trouble at home for something rather minor—not doing the dishes properly, forgetting to vacuum the basement—and I'd get yelled at or whupped. I'd bottle all of that dark energy within me and release it at school, getting into fights with classmates or cursing out teachers. The school would notify my dad, which would only get me in trouble back home. The more he beat on me, the more trouble I would get into at school. I had gotten kicked out of preschool (think about that . . . that's pretty hard to do). I got kicked out of elementary school. Home was no longer a safe space I could run back to. It was just an integral part of what kept the vicious cycle going.

Right before my dad got sick, my parents had bought a plot of land in East Hampton, out near the east end of Long Island. (Yes, *those* Hamptons.) They purchased the property so that my brothers and I could go to school out there, in what was a much better district. For a while, all we had there was a mailbox. My mom would drive us one and a half hours each way to get us to and from school every day. After nearly two years of commuting, we did build a modular home on the land and move there, with all of us pitching in on the construction of the house—the flooring and the Sheetrock and the retaining wall.

East Hampton was nothing like Coram, which was diverse. There were people from all over the world there, immigrant families like ours. East Hampton was pretty much the opposite. There were very few brown faces in town or in the schools. But my parents believed that putting us in a different—and much better—school system was important, that it would help all of us, and especially me.

Their plan, for me anyway, did not work. Not too long after we moved to East Hampton, I started hanging out with an older, faster crowd. I'd always been someone who sought out older kids, maybe because my brothers were so much older than me. I started cutting classes and hanging out by the beach.

This did not help things at home. If my dad heard that I got into even the most minor type of trouble at school, I was in for it. I'd walk into the house and instead of saying hello, he'd tell me to get into the "horse stance," a martial arts position when you squat and hold your arms straight out from your body. And then I'd take a beating. And the vicious cycle was perpetuated. I continued to bring the anger I generated at home with me to school, where I would unleash it and, inevitably, create more trouble at home. The scraps with classmates, the run-ins with teachers, and my terrible grades eventually got me kicked out of my first school in East Hampton.

It wasn't always all bad, though. One of my dad's favorite hobbies was going clamming down by Three Mile Harbor, which was steps from our home. One of the best perks of living out east, at least for my father, was being able to get a residential permit to catch fish and other shellfish to eat. He could go on and on about the best clamming conditions and the best techniques. I'd help carry his tools and the bucket full of clams, and afterward, my dad would cook a feast for us, often inviting other family and neighborhood friends. Although I wasn't the biggest fan of getting in the water and digging for clams, I loved being out there with him because I knew it was one of the few remaining things that made him happy. Also, it meant I wasn't getting disciplined, which was nice for a change.

. . .

From the vantage point of two decades later, I see very clearly what happened to my dad. Getting sick, though it didn't kill him, was still a nearly mortal wound. He was forced to become a househusband while my mom became the provider, bringing in the money and putting food on the table. The fact that he came from the very proud, paternalistic Haitian culture only amplified the pain that came with that. It demolished his ego. He loved—and lived—to work, to grind. When that was taken away from him, he lost his dignity, too. Dignity is a dangerous thing to take away from anyone, especially someone as proud as my father.

Why does my dad hate me? This, in some ways, was the central question of my childhood, and one I had no answer for then. But I see now that he didn't really hate me—he hated his disease and how he felt it emasculated him. I have now come to terms with this. I have forgiven him. In fact, in some strange way, I am grateful for what he put me through. He broke me down to the point that, now, no one can break me. And I've learned vital lessons from how he handled, or mishandled, his pain, lessons that would eventually help me turn my life around.

I also see now that a big part of all of this was on me. My attitude, actions, and words didn't help anything. I was being selfish by acting out at school and not learning how—or even really trying—to figure out a way to deal with what was going on. I took the easy way out, blaming everyone but myself.

I wasn't even close to being capable of succeeding back then because I didn't even try—or even know how to try—to succeed. Trying starts with preparing. And I never prepared for anything.

• • •

Even though I hated my dad when I was younger, I've always respected him. And I've always listened to him. I didn't always hear him. But I listened.

One of the things I listened to over and over growing up was a phrase he used to say all the time, something he borrowed from someone along the way that was reinforced by his training in the navy: *If you fail to prepare, prepare to fail*.

I think this saying resonated for him in the way that it does for most people. It's about working hard and trying hard. So much of his life was about preparation: the training at boot camp and the everyday readiness—the drilling and the Standard Operating Procedures—that are an integral part of the military. He studied manuals and learned everything he could about oil tanks for his job. As a Haitian immigrant, he believed that failure was not an option, so he prepared.

I think he repeated this phrase to me because he witnessed what I went through as a child and on into early adulthood, where I rarely, if ever, prepared for anything—like schoolwork—and routinely failed as a result.

As I grew and matured, though, I started to realize that there are deeper meanings to this phrase, nuances that make it even more powerful. There are two significant meanings. The first is:

If you are not prepared, you will have a handy, built-in excuse when you inevitably fail.

We've all experienced the first one. As a kid, I wouldn't do my schoolwork and then I'd fail a test. I'd write it off and tell myself either that I would have aced it had I studied, or that I was going to get a failing grade anyway. I always had an excuse to fail. I blamed my dad. I blamed my teachers. I blamed the other kids in school. The one person I never blamed was the one person who wasn't preparing, who wasn't even trying to succeed: me.

We've all traveled this path. The easy way out. We don't do the necessary, but often difficult, work beforehand. And then we fail because of it. And then we bail ourselves out by telling ourselves that we weren't going to succeed anyway.

But when we do this, we only compound the problem. We don't do the preparation, we fail because of it, and then we make an excuse. That excuse makes it easier to not prepare the next time around. And we fail again. It becomes a habit.

Preparing means trying, giving effort, risking something— your time, your comfort. If you prepare—really prepare—and fail, it's OK because of the second meaning of this saying:

> If you are not prepared and you fail because of it, that failure will become a setback instead of what it could and should be: a learning experience and a stepping-stone to success.

This one is a bit more complicated. All failures, according to *The Merriam-Webster Dictionary,* are setbacks. But that's not the case. Not if you put in the preparation.

For a long time in my life, I was moving too fast, tripping all over myself. I wasn't taking the time to prepare, to put in the work. As a result, I wasn't learning a thing from my failures. I wasn't even understanding that I could and should be learning from my failures.

I played basketball growing up. Still do. I've always loved

the game, the physical movement, the teamwork. I had some natural ability—I could dribble and shoot and could see the floor well. But in high school, when I should have been reaching my highest potential, I didn't. The reason: I didn't apply myself the way I should have. I had a lot of bravado, making it seem like I was a badass on the court. But the truth was that I didn't have the confidence to put in the work to make myself a better player.

My basketball career was a lot like my relationship with my dad. If I'd had a little less of an ego, if I had realized my own faults, things could have been different. But I took the easy way out, which in the end made it all harder.

It all boiled down to my relationship with myself. I failed at giving myself permission to prepare and fail. I was so scared of failing that I didn't even try—in basketball, with my dad, in life. Instead, I directed all of my energy toward looking cool and acting as if I didn't care, trying to mask the fact that I was not really trying.

I was hiding out in plain sight.

The turning point for me in my life came when I did slow down and started to be courageous enough to prepare—for the task at hand, for the day. It's when I realized that if I prepared and failed, I wasn't a loser. I was a learner.

"Fail fast, fail now, fail here, fail forward."

You've heard this advice before. It was the mantra of Silicon Valley in the late 1990s and early 2000s. It is absolutely terrible advice if you don't do the necessary preparation beforehand. Failing for the sake of failing nets you nothing. But if you prepare?

Then any failure you have is something you can learn from and make work *for* you, not against you.

Life is about experiencing things and learning about ourselves at every given opportunity. In order to do that, we must try, we must prepare. Jay-Z has a line in "Beach Chair" that goes: "I'm not afraid of dying, I'm afraid of not trying / Every day hit every wave like I'm Hawaiian."

You hear all the time that people get comfortable with failing in their lives, and that's why we fall into ruts. That's true to an extent. It happens when we don't prepare and try, and then fail, which yields the same built-in excuse I used to use ("I would have aced that test had I studied"). The bigger issue—what's really happening—is that we become *uncomfortable* with failing after we really try. When we prepare and try and still fail, we've lost all of our excuses. And that leads to discomfort. But that feeling of discomfort is what we have to get used to.

If we prepare, we will still fail sometimes. That's just how it goes. Basketball stars LeBron James, Steph Curry, and A'Ja Wilson are well-known for their meticulous workouts and game preparation. They still miss shots and lose games. But because they've put in the work, they're able to learn things that make them better the next time around.

If we are willing to prepare and fail, we will learn something. Learn what to do and learn what not to do. We will learn how to adapt and adjust.

We must get comfortable with that type of failing. Again, I'm not suggesting we *try* to fail. I'm suggesting we prepare, try, and if and when we do fail, learn from it.

Doing this is an expression of belief. We believe we can do something, so we prepare for it. If we fail, that's OK, because we believed. If we believe, we will learn. And with belief comes confidence.

There are thousands of practical applications here for all of us. Let's say we're trying to get in shape—lose weight, get heart-healthy. Whatever the reason. We decide to take up jogging. So we prepare. We get some running shoes, good ones that will help prevent injury. We get the outfit. We download an app and map out some jogging routes. We run a couple of times . . . and then we skip a day. And then another. And then another. Soon, we've stopped completely. In other words, we've failed.

But we *did* try. We prepared. That means we can learn from that failure; we can analyze how we can do a better job the next time. Did we get lazy? Did we not get enough sleep? We allow ourselves that failure because we can learn from it. Which makes it easier to try again.

Let's say we want that promotion at work. We study what the new job entails. We work on our pitch to our boss, practicing it over and over. We think long and hard about ourselves, analyzing our strengths and even our weaknesses. And then we go in and present our case . . . and we don't get it. That hurts. Always does and always will. But because we really tried and really prepared and really analyzed ourselves and challenged ourselves and put ourselves on the line, we learned some truly valuable things that will help us immensely in the long run. And we are better prepared for next time, when we will try again.

I prepare and fail—and learn—every day. I prepare my ass off for my Peloton classes. I start the preparation the night before, putting together a list of songs that mesh with the type of class I'm teaching (HIIT, Tabata, Climb, Club Bangers, Hip-hop, etc.). When I have the playlist down, I memorize it, listening to it and working through it before I go to bed. And then I work through it another three times in the morning before the class, nailing the time codes, the transitions, and the cadence for when the music amps up on a climb and when it chills out for a cooldown. Though I have it all down by then, I play it one more time in the car on my way to the studio while visualizing the entire Peloton ride. The car is a great place to practice at game speed because I have to concentrate on a bunch of different things (like driving) at the same time, like I do in class.

In the studio, I know what my cues are, where my cameras are, and exactly what every producer and camera operator is supposed to be doing. (Part of LeBron, Steph, and A'Ja's preparation, by the way, is knowing what each of their teammates is supposed to do, as well.) This is all part of my mental preparation. I have to be physically prepared, too, of course, so I stay in shape by working out and taking the time to recover on my off days. My regimen these days goes something like this: I train with weights three times a week and I do some serious cardio—like running on a treadmill—three days a week, mixed in with my classes. I make sure that I get rest between classes and workouts, and always take at least a day to totally chill, which includes getting off my feet and doing some cryotherapy and thermotherapy.

By the time the class begins, I am fully locked in and ready to execute. I am prepared so I can learn.

I prepare so diligently so that I don't need a script for class. I instruct from an authentic place and use my emotions that day to find the words I'm going to say. My preparation allows me to riff and freestyle. It's a bit like a jazz musician, who knows all of the notes and knows what every other bandmate is doing so that when the time comes for a riffing solo, she's ready to push herself to a place she's never been before. That riffing is the magic, that *feel*, that thing we all strive for when everything comes together to create a masterpiece. I can only reach that place when I have prepared for it.

Here's the thing, though. I still sometimes fail. Even after I've memorized the playlist and done all of the necessary work beforehand, I can still mess it up. I stutter or mumble my words. I miss a cue.

But I'm not afraid of that failure. I am willing to fail because I have prepared enough to push myself and my riders, and because I am learning from each and every one of those failures and getting better all the time. You can, too.

CHAPTER 2

THIS AIN'T DAY CARE

My classes are known for being tough. That's done on purpose. Remember, the classes are merely proxies for real life. They are practice, meant to get us all "in shape" for what's going to hit us out in the real world. And we need that practice. Because the real world is also tough. It doesn't discriminate. It doesn't matter how successful we are, how large (or small) our bank accounts are, how fit and healthy we are . . . the real world will dole out pain.

So, yes, the classes are tough. But, importantly, they are not impossible. In practicing for reality, we do something that's vital: We learn how to handle the pain, absorb it, and then—most important—how to turn it on its head and make it work *for* us, not against us. The real world is the same way—it's tough but also not impossible, not if and when we figure out how to navigate it.

This is a big concept that I didn't understand at all for most of my life. But when it finally clicked for me, everything changed.

. . .

My parents had purchased that plot of land in East Hampton for everyone, but they really had me in mind. A better school, a change of scenery—all of that was supposed to help me get my act together. It didn't. The trouble I was getting into out of school was escalating rapidly, especially because I was hanging out with the older crowd. And the problems I was causing in school had come to a head—there's not much use in being enrolled in a better school if you get kicked out of it, which I did. For my dad, that was the last straw. He saw no other option but to send me away to a place where he thought he could buy time for me, where I would be trapped, where you followed the rules or you paid for it, dearly. And that's how I ended up being sent to military school.

So, let's pick up where we left off there. I'm now fifteen, a little more than three-quarters of the way through my freshman year, which means I've somehow made it through nearly four years of military school. My parents had come to visit me twice during my time there. Their visits brought me a tiny sliver of joy. I was excited to see my mom, and she was excited to see me. My dad remained cold during those visits and didn't talk much, but just his presence brought some sense of normalcy. I even had some family at the school for a short time—my middle brother, Phil, did a postgrad year there. But postgrads had a different life at the school—they were separated a bit and didn't have to go through the humiliating things that us RATs did. So, though it was a good feeling to know that he was physically present there, I rarely saw him, and his year there went by in a flash.

Through nearly four years, military school had not broken me—my dad had already done that. In fact, I had gotten a helluva lot tougher with each year. But it was all still excruciating. I honestly don't know how I did it. It only feels real to me now because of the way I have come to use it.

Just as I was nearing the end of my freshman year, I got news that my maternal grandfather in Haiti had died. My grandparents had always been a huge part of my life, one of the few bright spots of my early years. I had a special bond with all of them. We'd traveled to Haiti a few times when I was younger, and it had helped me understand, at least a little, where I was from, what helped shape me, and why my parents were the way they were. All of my grandparents, like my parents, were no-nonsense and believed in always doing the right thing. But they doted on me. No tough love from them.

It was a big deal when my grandfather died. Paying my respects to the man meant a lot to me. I asked the school if I could go to the funeral. They said no. Their excuse was that I had too many sticks. And what they said went, full stop. They had complete control over me. My parents had signed over my parental rights. It made me feel helpless and angry—and even angrier at my dad, who had put me in this situation in the first place. So, instead of going to my grandfather's funeral, I marched tours on the quad all weekend.

That was my breaking point. A few weeks later, I decided that I had to get out of there. I just couldn't do it anymore. I called my parents and asked them to come get me, telling them that this time, I was dead serious. They said no. I felt stone cold inside.

I went to bed that night and decided that if my parents

would not come get me, I was going to force my way out. The next morning, I set out to do the only thing that was within my power—break every protocol I could and make it so that the school had no other option *but* to kick me out.

I cut classes. I got into some fights. I told my superiors to fuck off. In the process, I believe I set a record for sticks—I got 480 of them, more than ever humanly possible to march off. No one thing I did was really huge—I didn't want to do something so dumb that I'd regret it later. But every little act of defiance accumulated into a greater whole. Even though I was paying for it—getting smoked daily and marching tours nearly every free moment, I didn't care. I was disrupting my company, interrupting the drills, distracting the drill sergeants. I was not buying in to the program. In doing so, I was becoming a headache for the school, messing up their programming, and distracting the other cadets who they were trying to get to buy in. In retrospect, it was a pretty genius plan. Most of all because it worked.

I remember I was in math class one day when two officers knocked on the door and walked into the room.

"Toussaint, say your goodbyes."

After everything I'd been through, that was it. I walked out of the classroom with them to my room, where I packed up all of my belongings in about fifteen minutes. One of the officers drove me to the bus station.

"Your dad will be picking you up at the airport," he said as he handed me a bus ticket and a plane ticket.

Oh, shit, I thought. I hadn't really thought through what would happen if my plan actually worked.

I took the hour-long bus ride to the Kansas City Airport, flew to Midway in Chicago, and then had a connecting flight to MacArthur Airport on Long Island. My dad was waiting when I landed like the officer said he would be. He didn't utter a word to me when he picked me up or on the drive home. I had put my earrings in when I left school, yet another act of defiance. I wanted to piss my dad off as much as possible. It didn't have the intended effect, though. He didn't say anything about them. In fact, he didn't even appear to notice them.

My mom wasn't home when we got back. By that time, she was spending the weekdays living an hour and a half away with her sister in Amityville so she could be closer to her job in Queens and was home only on weekends. My brothers had both graduated from high school and were out of the house in college. It was now pretty much just my dad and me.

On my first morning back home, I woke up late and walked downstairs and passed by him. He didn't say a word or even acknowledge that I was there. *So this is how it's going to be*, I thought. *I can play that game, too.*

From that point on, for more than half a year, my dad and I lived together, saw each other every day, and never spoke more than just a passing word to each other. In the car. During dinner. Silence.

I was good at this game because military school had taught me one big thing: discipline. I could go for an extremely long time without speaking unless spoken to. My dad had the same level of discipline, of course. We were both stubborn as mules. In fact, we are a lot alike, which is maybe one of the reasons why we clashed so much. Even my mom couldn't break the silent standoff when she was home, though she and my dad did spend a lot of time fighting about it.

After about eight months of this détente, the ice finally broke, at least a little. Around Christmastime, my parents and I drove down to Virginia to visit family. During our stay, one of my aunts, Tati Momo, had observed how my dad and I interacted (or didn't). And just before we were about to leave to go back home, she grabbed both of us by the hand and stood there, looking into our faces, and pleaded with us to quit acting this way, for the sake of the family. It was sort of like an intervention. She started to cry, and then my dad did, too. It was the first time I'd ever seen him cry or show even a sliver of vulnerability.

Afterward, my dad and I did begin to talk to each other a little bit, mainly simple civilities. The ice was broken, yes, but our relationship remained arctic cold.

• • •

It would take a while, but there would come a time when I would use my experience at military school in a positive way. That happened when I figured out how to align the mental and physical aspects of my life to defeat the negative patterns I had been stuck in.

The first important lesson that military school taught me was that ***this ain't day care***.

Life is challenging. *And that's exactly how we should want it to be.*

It's human nature to want to get babied, to take the path of least resistance, to reap rewards without doing the work. I know this, because sometimes I want it this way, too.

But that's not how living in this world works. It can get rough out there. Nobody is going to pat us on the back all the time. We shouldn't want it that way, anyway.

The focus and determination to work—and not just cruise by—are the hallmarks of a real life with real meaning. We earn the results we get that way. And nobody can do this but us.

People come to my Peloton classes to hit their own PRs and ride that momentum into their real lives. I come to the classes to motivate people, to help them tap into whatever it is that gets them moving in the right direction. Outside motivation is incredible. And it works. Outside motivation can break up the inertia. But outside motivation can take us only so far. Once we start moving, the rest of the journey is up to us. Ultimately, my job is to provide you with the tools and the resources in order to find motivation for the big game of life, to get you to a point where you can find the hustle needed for the rest of your journey on your own.

I am motivated by the opportunity I have to wake up and go to work and do something I love, because there was a long time when I didn't have that opportunity. I am motivated to do the best I can on the bike, because I know there are people on the other side of the camera who are counting on me. I'm motivated by knowing that while we all are moving in place, we are going so far. I am motivated in knowing that I can help provide inspiration, help people believe they can accomplish something they didn't know they could. I'm there to help. But I can't want it for my riders more than they want it for themselves. I can't make my riders push themselves harder on a climb, for instance. They have to do it themselves. My mantra at the beginning of every class is this: "I'll provide the motivation. You give me the hustle, the dedication, and the focus."

It's the same thing in life. No one can do the work for us. No one can prepare for us. No one can fail and learn from that failure for us. No one can earn it for us. No one else can make us feel good inside. "You are responsible for your life," as Oprah Winfrey once said. "If you're sitting around waiting on somebody to save you, to fix you, to even help you, you are wasting your time. Only you have the power to move your life forward."

In my classes, once we've made it through the ride—the warmup, the climbs, the intervals, the cooldown—and once people have pushed themselves to reach personal records, I look directly into the camera and say:

"Way to work. *You* did that."

Because it's true.

But the riders don't need my validation. I'm just there to help us realize that if we believe in ourselves and do the work, others will notice and, more importantly, *we* will.

• • •

Military school provided me with that slap in the face, the realization that it was up to me. It also taught me some other very useful things, as well. I wasn't conscious of all of that learning and I certainly wasn't emotionally equipped to process it at the time. But the learning was there.

What I would realize later is that one of the biggest things I learned was how to survive, to be resilient in the face of what appears to be a hopeless situation. I hardened my body and my mind. I learned how to be mentally strong and how to use a form of meditation to get through the many hours I marched off sticks. I'd get so deep into the repetition and my isolation and breathing that I could hear birds landing on nearby branches during some of my marches. I developed an understanding of how to be comfortable by myself, in my own head.

I also learned how to count time, about cadence, and how to use my voice in an authoritative manner. I learned that practicing at game speed—"High Speed Low Drag"—was the best way to prepare for real life. All of these things would help me immensely later in life.

The actual pain would help, too. What I came to realize was that the most painful things that happened to me in my life— military school and my relationship with my dad—have made me that much tougher. Those things had knocked me down, dismantled me, piece by piece. But, in the end, I built myself back up and made myself stronger and sturdier than I ever have been.

We do this same thing, on a microlevel, in my classes. On the ride, we break ourselves down, physically and mentally, and we survive. We all do this when we push ourselves, whether that's in a workout, in the work required to sustain and strengthen our relationships within our families and with our loved ones or at our jobs, or really through any challenging or difficult situation we've faced and lived through. It's through sheer determination and fortitude that we build ourselves back up. Going through that process helps us build our self-confidence. It makes us feel good about ourselves. In my classes, we have worked the body. But we have really worked the mind. When we prove to ourselves that we can get broken down and then build ourselves back up, we realize that what seemed impossible was just a self-imposed limitation caused by self-doubt. We can apply that same lesson to our relationships, our jobs, and our lives. It changes our perspective on everything.

My experiences with my dad and in military school also provided me with a hard, indestructible shell. That shell protects me from being fazed by anything going on in the outside world. The only thing it didn't protect me from was the pain I felt inside. At some point, I had to acknowledge the pain I felt. But by finally acknowledging the pain, I no longer allowed it to have control over me. Instead, *I* control *it*.

The key here is to ***turn your pain into power***.

Bad and painful things happen to all of us. They happen to billionaires. They happen to people who struggle to make the monthly rent payment. There isn't a person in the world who hasn't gone through *some* shit in their lives. Life isn't fair. It doles out pain to everyone without bias. Always has and always will.

One of my best friends lost *both* of his parents to terminal illnesses within a span of five years. He was in his teens at the time. Somehow, someway—I think by keeping his faith, keeping his feet on the ground, and staying true to his purpose—he made it through. Look, he was in real pain. I saw that. But he battled, and even his down days were better than most people's good ones. I watched him wake up every single day and still manage to move forward. He never lost his light, never let anything become an excuse to give up or abuse substances or himself. He has always been an inspiration to me.

The key is to not let that pain control us or paralyze us. Don't let it rob us of our light. But don't ignore it, either. Instead, assign it a purpose—turn it into a source of power and positive energy. If we don't do this, we'll be stuck in whatever hole it put us into in the first place.

This transformation of pain into power is a fundamental part of feeling good about ourselves.

I do this now with all of the failing-and-not-learning-from-it I did early in my life, and with military school and my dad. I acknowledge and process the pain. I remind myself that I survived it and overcame it and use that reminder to spark a fire of motivation within me when I need it. Military school made me stronger, but only because I assigned it that purpose. My relationship with my dad made me more open and aware, but only because I assigned it that purpose. I continue to deal with all the bad, painful things that come my way in the same manner.

All pain comes with something learned. We examine the pain. Process it. And then focus on what we learned from it, and allow that to motivate us and push us and strengthen us.

But how do we go about examining and processing that pain and any other emotions, for that matter?

One thing I've learned over the years as an instructor is that I have to be in the right frame of mind when I leave the house to go teach a class. I don't have to be perfect, but I can't be down or angry or distracted. Otherwise, I bring that energy to class and screw up the entire experience, for the riders and for me.

The way I deal with it is to stop and take some time for myself before I head out of the door. I do this every day. You have to set aside time to *be present with yourself*. We can't provide light to anyone else unless we first provide light to ourselves. In that way, being present with ourselves is a form of selfless selfishness.

Being present with ourselves (and that selfless selfishness) is a big part of feeling good, this ability to recognize and deal with what's going on within us. It's not a permanent state, of course. We don't just do it once and have it all figured out for good. We have to work on it every day. That may sound tedious and too difficult, but it's not. The process builds discipline. And the discipline gives us the power.

We have to stop what we're doing every day and recognize and acknowledge the negative—and yes, the positive—feelings that are within us. I find that it's especially important to do this in the morning, before we begin to tackle the day. Are we feeling great, like we're ready to kick ass and take on the world? Excellent. It's still worth thinking through why we feel that way and how we got there, so it can become repeatable. And then process those good vibes, own them, and get out there and ride it all day.

But it's maybe more important to do all of this when we're not feeling all that great. Recognize and acknowledge that, too. And then open yourself up to thoughts, priorities, and actions that might help you fix it. There's beauty in the effort, the mindful attempt to figure it out. Just going through this process can help us get back—or stay—on track.

I did this during the heart of the pandemic, that first winter when there was no end in sight to the lockdowns and closed businesses, mixed with fear and apprehension and loneliness. I recognized the feelings I was having and acknowledged them. I even said them out loud to myself a few times. And then I took some time to think and focus on what was making me feel this way, and what I could control about it and what I could not. I addressed it head-on. I owned it and ran toward it. Running away from it would have only made it worse in the end. Those emotions would have found me eventually, and they would have grown in power from the neglect. This simple, mindful exercise helped me get through those tough days and months. I thought about myself, accepted that it was OK to feel out of sorts. I thought about ways to get myself back on track, like staying disciplined with my workouts, keeping to a routine, and talking frequently with my family and friends. And I made sure to take time to just let myself chill, and trust me, I did just that. (I rose to the top division in NBA 2K online play. Find my gamer tag if you want the smoke.)

It can be extremely difficult to be present with ourselves. Most days, we rush out of the door, anxious, caffeinated, and amped up about the day. Our lives, particularly now with the constant connection (and disconnection) of our phones, can be dizzying. It's much easier to bury our feelings in the rush and not deal with them, not take the time. But we're all Cinderella before her carriage turned into a pumpkin if we do that. The clock will strike midnight at some point, and we'll be exposed.

There is a physical way to start to be present with ourselves, which involves breath work, but with a stated purpose. That is, you have to *inhale your confidence and exhale your doubt*.

I've made this part of my morning ritual that helps me be present with myself. My eyes open when I wake up. My feet touch the ground. I stand in front of the mirror, close my eyes, and do three "inhale your confidence and exhale your doubt" breaths. And I mean I *do* them, with concentration and focus. On the third one, I inhale and then open my eyes and then yell as loud as I can as I exhale, consciously forcing out the bad energy.

Part of this comes from my experience at military school. When a drill sergeant asks you a question, you can't just answer with a limp "yes, sir." You have to yell it with a purpose: "YES, SIR!" And during our cadet workout sessions, we yelled as we lifted weights and ran countless sprints. We are human. We all have energy that exists within us every day, both negative and positive. The yelling can release the negative shit in your mind and body and activate the positive stuff. Consciously—and physically—releasing the negative energy sets us up with a new vibe, resets our levels. (Sound a bit crazy? Try it.)

This daily ritual works a lot of the time for me (and probably occasionally freaks out the neighbors, though my two dogs have gotten used to it). But sometimes, the stress remains, refuses to be expelled. If that happens, I double down on being present with myself. I stop what I'm doing—taking the time here is critical—and force myself to take a moment to acknowledge the stress and try to get to the root cause of it. I try to figure out a way to attack the problem and consciously change and protect my energy so I don't carry it with me out of the door, so I don't bring it with me to class, to my interactions with my business team or colleagues or even to the baristas at Starbucks. Sometimes just the act of going through it—the process—helps.

But other times, even that doesn't work. Most of the time, it doesn't work when I have to deal with a bigger problem that hits close to home, maybe within my family, or with my friends, or with work.

A few years ago, I came up with a rule for addressing these bigger problems. At the time, I was coming off a long and mostly great relationship. The end was extremely painful, though, and it lingered because I didn't want to face it.

These types of problems require a bigger space to work through them. I give myself two days, which is why I call it *the 48-hour rule*.

In giving myself forty-eight hours to deal with the problem, I take a little of the pressure off. I have allowed myself time. But that doesn't mean that I can just cruise through the process or become passive. The time needs to be used wisely and productively.

During those forty-eight hours, I disconnect as much as I can. I don't necessarily have to grind on the problem for the entire duration—in fact, I found that it's good to *not* think about the problem for long stretches at a time—but no good comes from just ignoring the problem in its entirety and thumbing through Instagram. I put the phone and computer away. I allow myself the time needed to feel it, to hurt.

I spend some of those hours sitting in a comfortable chair or even lying in bed and closing my eyes and thinking, getting into a quasi-meditative state. And I spend some of those hours moving my body—working out, going to a basketball court and getting some shots up. (Few things stimulate the mind better than a workout.) I find that it's important to do both of these things, to move your mind and body in an effort to align them.

I also give myself the grace to make and acknowledge mistakes and to learn from them. The Failing Fast principle—going for it (in other words, *trying*) with an open and free mind, now and not later—is about providing yourself with the space to fail and learn. Maybe I'm somehow responsible for causing this problem I'm dealing with, maybe I haven't fully considered other perspectives and viewpoints, maybe I need to check my ego. . . .

And, usually, if I've put in the time and the work, after forty-eight hours, I'm back on point.

I've found that forty-eight hours is usually the perfect amount of time for these bigger problems. It lets the raw emotions recede, and gives enough time to engage the intellect, in conversations with ourselves and with others. The timing on this may be different for you. Nick Saban, the University of Alabama football coach, has what he calls his "24-hour rule," in which he gives his team that amount of time to celebrate a victory or mourn a loss. After that, they move on to the next game. Maybe that's enough time for you? Or maybe you need more than forty-eight hours? It doesn't really matter. What matters is doing it.

Now, sometimes we don't have forty-eight continuous hours (or whatever time you've determined is right for you) to spare. We have work commitments, kid duty, life. If we don't have forty-eight straight hours, that's OK. We can carve out the time whenever we can, and piece it together if need be. The important thing is doing the work, not necessarily *when* you do the work. In the end, one of the best things about the 48-hour rule is that the better you get at doing it, the less you have to actually use it.

All of this—turning our pain into power, being present

with ourselves, allowing ourselves the time to work through problems—are keys to feeling good. All of it works to instill inner confidence and strength, qualities that, when developed, allow us to move with clarity and decisiveness. That self-confidence and strength give us protection, almost like an acquired immunity. We get mentally stronger, and certain things—like those silly issues that pop up periodically and bother us—just can't reach us like they used to. We grow more powerful and, in doing so, sap the negativity around us of its strength.

Again, though, it took me years to figure this out about myself. And the lessons came the hard way.

CHAPTER 3

THE PATH

Gratitude is something I talk and think about a lot. These days, it's a word that's tossed around carelessly, to the point of nearly becoming a hollow cliché. But I think it's worth pushing past the cliché and seriously contemplating what the word really means.

Gratitude is something that comes from within, something that we feel inside. It's a crucial part of our interiority that can, somewhat paradoxically, free us from some of the pitfalls of being *too* stuck inside our own heads. Gratitude unlocks something within us, helping to remove and overcome our own fear and negative thoughts and energies. It is one of the most important tools we have for getting out of a rut or a hole.

Finding—and then activating—our gratitude is a significant part of being present with ourselves. It can be found and activated by some of the smallest things—again, these may seem like clichés, but just try them. Think about the food you have in your fridge and the roof you have over your head. Think about your kids and how much you love them. Think about your dog and how much he loves you. Think about the opportunity you are given each and every day just through the simple act of waking up. If you are reading this line in this book right now, you can find some gratitude, because you are breathing, you are alive. You are blessed.

Gratitude helps us move toward feeling good. It is the bridge between doubt and belief. Walk—no, run!—across it. Gratitude is the foundation we create to cancel out negativity and fear. When we remove those two emotions, we have cleared the path across that bridge. There is work that still needs to be done—there always will be—but by feeling gratitude, we've removed the resistance.

Practicing gratitude is hard. We might not be good at it at first. That's why it's called *practice*. We wake up, sit on the edge of our beds, breathe, and think about the simplest thing we can that we are grateful for—our job, our kids—whatever it is. That slight pause of awareness, that gets it going. It's a mind hack. That little pause shifts perspective. It's a small step, but those small steps take us long distances. We get better at practicing gratitude through repetition, I promise. Do it day after day, and it will open up our minds just a bit more and let in more light.

One of the keys is to do it like everything else we do: at game speed. With intensity. Don't just breeze over thinking about your food or your kids or your dog. Do it with some passion and depth, with concentration and focus. Practicing gratitude is an active experience, not a passive one.

Now, I know it can be hard to find and activate. We all get

stuck in our negative headspace—that unappreciative email from our boss, that asshole on the road who cut us off, that Instagram post by a friend that made us feel left out or uncool or small. We can so easily get anxious and overcome with worry and doubt and negativity.

Sometimes, it can feel like there's no way we can find our gratitude, even through the little things. We all feel this way. So, what to do?

I've found that when this happens, it almost always helps to think about other people in our lives and the things they have done to help us. I've been blessed to have many people support me along my journey.

• • •

After getting kicked out of military school at what was basically the end of my freshman year, I enrolled as a sophomore at East Hampton High School, where my mom had taught years before. I continued to struggle with school—getting terrible grades, cutting classes. I was still stuck in that vicious cycle of bad things at school resulting in bad things at home, which resulted in more bad things at school. Rinse. Repeat. My dad and I were on speaking terms, yes, but it mostly consisted of him yelling at me and me talking back to him. Failing at school made me feel horrible about myself. My dad made me feel worse. He was still very disappointed and angry that I had gotten kicked out of military school. He had run out of options for buying me time.

About halfway through my junior year, I managed to fuck things up even more. One day, at school, I somehow got my hands on a string of firecrackers. I knew nothing about them, really. I'd never even seen them before. I thought it would be funny to light them. So I went to the end of the main hallway in school and did just that. The noise of all of the firecrackers going off scared the shit out of me. It reverberated in the hallway. The noise scared the shit out of everyone else, too.

While there were certainly many teachers who believed that I should have been kicked out of school right away, that didn't happen. My saving grace was the respect that some of the people in the administration had for my mom when she had taught there. Instead, I was suspended for the remainder of the year. I spent my days at home, trying to avoid my dad. In the late afternoons, I went to the library where a few of my teachers taught me after the school day was over (another courtesy gained from my mom). Getting suspended and being home all day only heightened my dad's anger toward me. And those firecrackers reignited the worst stuff between us.

During these years in high school, I developed a few ways of coping with the misery I was feeling. After school, during the time I wasn't suspended, I was strategic about how I walked into the house if my dad was at home. If I thought he was in the kitchen when I arrived, I'd enter through the basement. If I could see him in the living room through the front window, I'd sneak into the side door and sprint up to my room. I did anything to postpone the inevitable clash with him as long as I could.

A lot of times, though, I'd just put off going home altogether. My after-school bus dropped me off a few blocks from my house. The normal walk home took five minutes. I could add another ten minutes if I took the long way, which I often did. But other times, I wouldn't go home at all, not right away. I'd instead walk to a little path on my street that led down to the water at Three Mile Harbor. The path was grassy and shaded by big trees. There were cattails as you got closer to the water.

There weren't too many places you could walk around as a Black kid in East Hampton without raising suspicion. There was even a woman in our neighborhood who periodically called the cops on me, even after we'd lived there for years. The first time she did it, I'd been playing in the street in front of her house for a while. I'd gone home, where my dad told me to vacuum the basement. I was down there when a cop walked right up to the door and scared the shit out of me and asked to see my dad. Her calling the cops on me was something I wouldn't really confront until much later in my life. The suspicion I raised with my mere presence is something I wasn't really aware of back then. A blissful ignorance given what I now know.

But this path was well out of that neighbor's sight, hidden. It was my secret place where I never saw anyone else. I spent a lot of time down there—I would also use it as a refuge after a bad confrontation at home or school. Being there reminded me a bit of the marching tours I did at military school. It was quiet. I'd force myself to sit still and literally stare over the water for hours. (I didn't have the distraction of a phone at the time.) Sometimes, I'd skip rocks or shells.

It was down by that water where I had some of my darkest thoughts. I wondered what it would be like just to walk out into the water and not turn back. I wondered if anyone would really give a shit if I were gone, because I seemed to make so many people around me miserable, mostly myself. I cried a lot down there.

But luckily, I had another way to cope, which may have saved my life. It came in the form of a great friend.

• • •

At this point in my life, there had been a handful of people who helped me or looked out for me for no real reason other than they noticed that I just seemed to need it. Because of the trouble I always found, I wasn't the easiest kid to go to bat for. And yet, some people just showed up for me.

If I had been really paying attention or had been better equipped emotionally, I would have expressed gratitude to all of these people for what they did for me. I didn't at the time, of course. Thankfully, that didn't seem to matter to them.

Susan Verde was my kindergarten teacher at Hampton Day School in Bridgehampton. We were still living in Coram at the time but had the property in East Hampton so I could go to school out there, one and a half hours away. I was restless and antsy at this time of my life—and I've always learned better while moving and playing rather than when sitting at a desk. I would frequently show up at school in the mornings tired because of how early I had to wake up to make it there on time. I had also left my preschool in Coram, where there were a lot of kids and teachers who looked like me, to attend a school that was 99 percent white. Kids are usually great at those types of adjustments, particularly young kids, who don't even seem to see color. But the otherness is still felt.

Ms. Verde was always there for me. She made sure I had room to roam and play and made me feel seen and safe. She also had that sixth sense that all great teachers seem to possess. She understood that I needed a little something else, as well, so she made it a point to hug me many times throughout the day.

My guidance counselor in middle school in the Hamptons also had my back. When I was in fifth grade, before I went to military school, I started running around with an older crowd made up of sixth and seventh graders, at lunch and recess, after school. I was just trying to find my tribe in this new school and place. At first, I was merely on the periphery of the group, but as the school year went on, I inched my way closer to the core. These guys were a lot more mature than I was, and their idea of fun was to egg each other on to do crazy and sometimes stupid things. Smash mailboxes. Steal candy. That sort of thing.

My guidance counselor observed what was happening. Now, this guy had *no* reason on earth to do anything nice for me. I was a bad student. I talked back to teachers. I cut classes. I was disruptive in school. But he did something for me, anyway, and I'll never know why.

One day he called me into his office. He told me that he knew what was going on, that I felt cool and included when I hung out with these older kids. But he warned me that they didn't necessarily have my best interests at heart, and that some of them were headed for real trouble—with the police, with jail—and that I was going to be dragged into it if I wasn't careful. He knew that I didn't have a great relationship with my dad, but still had a level of respect for him. He asked me to think about how angry my dad already was at me when I got into relatively minor trouble, and what possible heights that anger would reach if I ever got into real trouble.

His words hit home. I gradually started to peel myself away from the older crowd and, eventually, quit hanging out with them altogether. Now, my guidance counselor couldn't save me from getting kicked out of that school and being sent to military school. No one could have done that but me. But he did save me from getting a record, which almost certainly would have happened if I'd kept hanging around those kids. Many of them did end up getting arrested for one reason or another. Some of them even ended up in juvenile detention. I was never a good kid and I got into a lot of petty trouble, but I avoided the really bad stuff, thanks in large part to my guidance counselor.

I even had someone look after me in military school, even though nothing I did there made me deserving of any help.

My first meeting with Captain Ragsdale was super awkward. It was at my first meal at the school, on the day when my parents dropped me off and I had gotten smoked on the quad. With my stomach still burning, someone introduced me to Captain Ragsdale. I stuck out my hand.

His face reddened with anger. "Don't you *ever* stick your hand out at me!" he yelled. "Do you know who you are talking to right now?"

I had no idea. But I'd learn right then and there that he was a captain and that I was supposed to salute him.

Captain Ragsdale was really tough on me. He was really tough on everyone. He drilled me. He smoked me. He gave me sticks. He forced me to conform to the school's training as much as I could. But, for some unknown reason, he also looked out for me.

Every once in a while, he'd come by my room. He'd usually yell at me or smoke me, but I could tell that there was something more to his visits.

In my second year at the school, he came by one day and told me to follow him. We walked to his room, where some other senior staffers were hanging out. I was initially a little scared of what they were going to do me, but then I realized there was a different vibe in the room. The staffers were playing cards and smiling. They had illicit candy and beer. There was a video game console set up that they'd snuck in and kept hidden. The room felt, well, a bit normal. It was like some alternate universe, a sanctuary, where the rules of the military school were temporarily suspended. No yelling. No getting smoked. No sticks.

I felt like I had been inducted into a secret society. I knew that if I ever talked about it, I'd get into serious trouble and, worse than that, would never be invited back. Kind of the *Fight Club* rule. So I never did.

And so, for one night about every two months, I got to chill and relax and act like a normal seventh grader with Captain Ragsdale and the others. Those nights were vitally important to me, giving me something to look forward to every day and keeping me somewhat sane. They were a big reason why I made it as long as I did at military school.

I first met William Hartwell in elementary school, where he was the gym teacher. I always thought he was really cool when I was a little kid—he got to dress in sweats, he actually talked to us kids like we were people, we called him "Coach," and he taught my favorite class. But it wasn't until I was older that he started to play a pivotal role in my life.

We stayed in touch as I went to middle school, military school, and even high school. Coach Hartwell was, essentially, a father figure to me. He always had the ability to read my vibe. When things got to their darkest point in my relationship with my dad, Coach Hartwell would somehow show up and ask me if I wanted to go shoot hoops or do something else. He was also there for me when my dad either couldn't show up, because of his health, or wouldn't show up, because of our frayed relationship.

Coach Hartwell and I talked a lot about my dad, and he shielded me from my most negative thoughts about him. He explained that, even at his worst, my dad still had my best interests at heart. My feelings toward my dad would have been a lot darker without Coach Hartwell. My feelings about myself would have been a lot darker, too.

Coach Hartwell did some dad-like things, like taking me to, and picking me up from, summer camp. But it was the life lessons he shared that had the most impact on me. He never preached. He let his actions speak for themselves. He was the first person who showed me what it was like to be a Black man in America, how to operate in society, and how and why to stay out of big trouble. Things my dad, as an immigrant, wasn't necessarily able to teach me. Coach Hartwell took me and a few other Black kids on a trip to walk across the Edmund Pettus Bridge in Selma, Alabama—where John Lewis and other civil rights leaders were beaten as they marched on what is now known as "Bloody

Sunday"—so I could feel the history and start to comprehend it. He was also one of the biggest influences on me when it came to wanting to give back to the community. When I was seventeen, he took a group of us down to New Orleans to help people clean up their houses after Hurricane Katrina, which opened up my eyes to the importance of service.

The significance of these people in my life cannot be over-stated. I really don't know if I would be around right now without them. And if you've ever wondered why I go out of my way to show love to all of the teachers and educators—with dedicated Peloton "teacher appreciation" rides and frequent shoutouts—this is why. I'll never forget the teachers who looked out for me beyond the classroom and curriculum, beyond their job description.

• • •

But one person has always stood out among all others. Up to this point in my life, no one in the world was there for me more times and in a more significant way than my friend Jerome.

I first met Jerome when I moved out to East Hampton, but I didn't really get to know him until high school, where he was a grade above me. He was one of the few other Black kids in town. Jerome was the youngest in his family. He always felt like a big brother to me, and I think he liked having someone around who was like a younger brother to him.

Whenever stuff at home got to the point where I couldn't handle it anymore and I felt too messed up to be alone at the water, I would call Jerome. Either he or his girlfriend at the time,

Jayvee—or, sometimes, both of them—would come pick me up. I never really cared what we did after they got me. It was enough just to be away from the house and my thoughts and with them. A lot of times, we just drove around town. We talked and we laughed. And I no longer felt alone.

My favorite times, though, were when we went to Jerome's house. It was just on the outskirts of town, a blue house not unlike mine or anyone else's to an outsider. But what made it different for me was that it wasn't just a house, it was a home.

Jerome's house was always bustling with activity—his siblings, parents, and various cousins were always in and out. I'd go over there and just hang out. No stress. No yelling, or at least no yelling with negative intent. We'd play video games and ride bikes. His mom, Sonja, fed us. She kidded us about existent or nonexistent girlfriends. She was always available to listen to me when I needed to talk about what was going on in my life. I cried a lot with her. Jerome's family wasn't the wealthiest in town by any means. But it was a family and a home that was richer in spirit, energy, and love than any I'd ever known.

My junior year I played on the varsity basketball team. It was a very good team that went 23–2 on the season. Jerome was the captain and the star player. I was just good enough to make the team and even contribute a bit to its success. My mom could never make my games because of her work during the week. My dad never showed up, not even once. But Jerome's parents did. They basically treated me as they did Jerome, as if I were another son. They'd bring me food before we played. They'd drive me home when the game was over. I don't know why they did what they did for me. But they helped me survive. And Jerome would continue to play a massive role in my survival as I got older.

I wish I could go back in time and express my gratitude to all of these people who selflessly helped me back then. Sure, it's never too late to say thank you, and I have said this since then to all of these folks. But the awareness and expression of gratitude at the time would have done me a world of good.

· · ·

Gratitude is the foundation of feeling good. Basically, it's sort of a chicken-and-egg thing. Gratitude comes when we feel good, and we feel good when we find it. Feeling and expressing gratitude is something we must do every single day. We can find it by thinking about the simple things that we are grateful for. We can find it by thinking about how others have helped us along the way. There are some other ways to access it, as well.

I have a phrase that I say to myself often, which touches on something I mentioned before: *Smile. You woke up today.*

The phrase came from my dad and my brother Phil. When we were kids, Phil would often wake up in a bad mood, which manifested as a grimace on his face. In hindsight, I realize now that he by no means *wanted* to start the day like that. But I remember when we sat at the breakfast table and my dad would turn to him and say, "Wipe that puss off your face, son. You woke up today."

I wanted Phil to smile, too. As a kid, seeing someone with that look on their face, even if that person can't help it, is draining.

We all wake up in bad moods. It just happens. But whenever I wake up tired, grouchy, sore, or angry, I remind myself to smile, because being able to have those feelings is a luxury. It's a privilege.

Because I woke up today. I've been given life, a new day, a fresh start, and the opportunity to do something great. Not everyone is so blessed. If I focus on the gratitude I have for that blessing—and not on the negative or on the things I do not have—I'm ready for the day and for all of the chances it will provide me to be great. Even if we find ourselves at what feels like rock bottom, we can find at least one thing we are grateful for and connect with it. And that often provides the spark, the first step to getting up off the floor.

Gratitude is a form of love, of self-love, really. If and when you feel that love, you feel good. And with that love, you have taken the first step needed to spread it.

Why is it important to share gratitude? Because the more blessings you give, the more you receive. In class, I give the love and I crave the love that is returned. Even if we think we're too selfish to feel love and spread it, just understand this: We always get it in return.

Love, in one way at least, is like money. If you invest it wisely, it grows. There is no return without investment.

In the mornings, after I've inhaled my confidence and exhaled my doubt, I concentrate on some things I feel grateful for (I do this when I brush my teeth). I think about my family, my friends, my health, my job, my dogs, that I made it through everything to get where I am now. It's an exercise done with serious intent. It takes only a moment. But it's vitally important because it orients my mental state. Because if you ***find your gratitude and fix your attitude, that will help you reach your greatest altitude***.

We create our own reality. So much of life is just what happens between our ears. How we view ourselves *is* our reality. Our attitude *is* our reality. One way to get the right attitude about ourselves is to express our gratitude. Attitude becomes a manifestation of gratitude.

For so long in my life, I didn't acknowledge my gratitude and express it. And that made me have a terrible attitude, toward the world and myself. I felt like the world was out to get me (it wasn't). I concentrated on all the things I thought I didn't have and never stopped to think about how lucky I was. It's never lost on me that I am the son of two Haitian immigrants who worked their asses off so that I would not only have an opportunity in life, but also a better one than they had. They provided me with a house, food, and the best schooling they could find, so many opportunities that others don't have in their lives. But I didn't realize this or figure it out for two decades. I was too caught up in my bad attitude. I wallowed in self-pity. It pains me now to think of how I took all of this for granted, to think about how many other people in this world would have traded places with me in a millisecond, people who have suffered great trauma, people without shelter or food.

We are all blessed in some way. Plenty of people out there would give it all to exchange positions with us. I felt J. Cole when he says, in "Love Yourz," that there's "no such thing as a life that's better than yours." It doesn't matter whether we are a pro athlete, a teacher, a soccer mom. We can all find our gratitude by being real with ourselves, by concentrating on the positive and pushing out the negative, by analyzing what's going on within us, what's dragging us down, what's pulling us up.

But this blessedness that we all have comes with a responsibility: We must own it, express it, and make the most of it by trying, by preparing.

Part of my transformation—when I started to feel good—came when I finally recognized and realized how blessed I was and how blessed I am. I finally found my gratitude. I had hit rock bottom and realized there was no other way to go than up.

CHAPTER 4

STOP EXISTING, START LIVING

At various points in our lives, we all put ourselves on cruise control. We don't hit the gas and accelerate. We don't pump the brakes to slow down. We just coast.

This is perfectly OK . . . in the short term. It's a break. We all need them.

But when we put ourselves on cruise control for a long time, we cede control, volition, and intention. We are merely existing.

"Existing" means barely getting by. It means we are not applying ourselves anywhere close to our max potential. It's not trying, not preparing, and failing without learning. It's not being present with ourselves. It's looking outside for validation of our own self-worth, and letting the insecurities and doubts of others put parameters on us. It's letting negativity linger and control us, as opposed to making it work for us. It's not controlling the narrative of our own lives. It's not feeling gratitude for all of the things we *do* have.

We have to *stop existing and start living*.

"Living" is about taking control of our own lives and not just letting it happen to us. It's about accelerating and braking when need be. It's about being present, with ourselves and others. It's about listening and processing and analyzing.

Live! Don't just passively and endlessly scroll through social media. We are the author of our own stories. Try. Prepare and live with intentionality. Living is about not letting opportunities just pass us by. It's about pushing ourselves.

I know all of this now. But it took a long time—and one event in particular—for me to get there.

• • •

When I started my senior year of high school, I decided that I really didn't want to get held back and prolong the agony of high school, which was a decent possibility at the time. Nothing like a little motivation. So I applied myself just enough to get by and graduate.

Now I had to make a decision about college. I didn't really want to go—school clearly wasn't for me. But I knew my parents wanted me to. Education was always a huge deal to them, especially, of course, to my mom. There also was some pressure on me, a high bar that I had to live up to. My oldest brother, Martial, my father's namesake, was the golden child. He had never gotten in trouble, and I felt like he could do no wrong. He was also a great student and had gone to Brown University, which made my parents ecstatic. Even Phil, after some ups and downs, had made it to college.

My parents hung on to that first-generation immigrant dream for all of us: We would get a good education, get a good, stable job, settle down and raise a family, so that their labors and sacrifices would be validated by our success.

It clearly wasn't working out like that for me. But college did sound intriguing to me for two important reasons: It would finally get me out of the house and it would buy me more time to try to figure things out.

I was eligible for college because I had a diploma from high school and because, as bad as I was as a kid, I did one critical thing right: I had never been arrested. Not having a record was actually a very important thing to me, as my middle school guidance counselor had surmised. Had I ever gotten arrested, my dad would have completely written me off, and the last thin thread that held our relationship together would have been severed. It had been harder to pull off than it sounds. First, I had no feelings of self-worth at all, and when that's the case, you end up doing the stupid "fuck it" kind of things that can get you in big trouble. Second, some of my friends had a record by our senior year, mostly from doing those stupid "fuck it" kind of things.

But while I could go to college, I had no idea where I wanted to apply. And I didn't have the grades to cast that wide a net.

I had a friend named Tafa Peters, who had been a year ahead of me at East Hampton High School. He had moved to the United States from Grenada when he was seven years old. After high school, Tafa had gone to college at New England Institute of Technology (NEIT), located on the outskirts of Providence, Rhode Island. He was studying music there. (He's since become the very successful musician known as T-Shyne.) Tafa knew that I, too, loved music. He also knew that I didn't want to take the SATs (and his school didn't require them). NEIT seemed like a great fit. Maybe the only fit. So I applied, got in, enrolled, then decided to study audio and video.

My dad was stunned that I got into *any* college. He thought for sure that there was no way that I'd make it that far, in education and maybe in life. He was so shocked that he rewarded me with the use of a hand-me-down car, one that had been driven by Martial while he was at Brown in Providence. It was a black Mercedes C230 Kompressor. It had some serious driving time on it, something like 220,000 miles. But the car meant a lot—despite the mileage, it was a cool ride. And it had come from my dad. He never actually verbalized that he was pleased with me, but this was his way of saying it, and it was the first piece of positive encouragement I had received from him since I was six years old.

I loved my first year in college. I was away from home and all of its dark clouds. And I truly applied myself in school for what was really the first time ever. I got good grades in most of my classes, especially in the audio and video ones. I learned how to set up A/V equipment—the wiring, the back-end stuff, the sound design. I was shooting projects and doing voice-overs. I had my own radio show. And I had even envisioned my dream job in my head: a broadcaster or camera operator at ESPN. Just for a moment, I felt like my life had found its track.

But then came my second year. I fell back into my old habits. I lost my focus. I started to party. A lot. My classes seemed harder and less interesting, so I began to skip them, a day or two to start, and then entire weeks. My parents had me on a $200-a-month allowance, which I more often than not used up in the first week because of the partying. I decided I needed more money, so I started doing something really stupid: selling weed. Well, it was more like I *tried* to sell weed. I ended up smoking most of my stash. I must have been the worst weed dealer ever. I couldn't even do that right. Remember that thing about learning from failure? The lesson here was that I was never going to get rich in this line of work.

I was so bad at it, in fact, I tempted fate. I was running out of money . . . and "work." The guys who I bought the weed from were getting pissed. The guys who I was supposed to be selling it to were also getting pissed.

And here's where Jerome came in to help me yet again. He was still back in East Hampton. But when he got wind of what I was doing, he realized that I was potentially putting myself in a really dangerous place. I mean, you don't want to get crosswise with people who deal drugs for a living.

He got in his car and drove up to see me.

Jerome knew this scene just wasn't me. He sat me down and told me that I had no business messing around in this game. And then he said something that has stuck with me ever since. "Lex, I can't let you keep doing this. You're going somewhere in life, I know it. I'm looking out for you because I know you'd do the same for me."

And then *he* put me on an allowance so I could stop selling weed. He had a steady job, and sent me money every two weeks. It was an incredible act of generosity and love. I didn't fully understand or appreciate all of what he did at the time. He believed in me before I believed in myself, saw a light in me that I couldn't see during those dark days. To this day, I think it's the most gangster move I've ever seen.

Jerome saved me from getting hurt or worse. He'd thrown me a lifeline. And yet, I still couldn't get it together, in school or otherwise. I couldn't get myself out of the deep, dark hole that I had once again dug myself into.

I dropped out of college. Just stopped going to class altogether. But I didn't tell my parents. Instead, I pretended that I was still going to class, still enrolled. For two months, every time they called, I told myself, *Today's the day I will tell them.* But I never did. And the longer I let the lie go, the further away I got from telling the truth.

Then my mom called one day. She told me that she had gotten a letter that my student loan was deactivated.

"I know what's going on, Lex," she said.

And then she told me that I—and not she—was the one who had to tell my father that I had dropped out of college. *Hell, no*, I thought. *I ain't doing that. Not after he was proud of me for the first time in my life.* I tried to run away and hide from the problem I had created, and it followed me, growing in strength like a hurricane. I didn't plan to tell my dad anything until I was forced to do so.

A week after my mom called, I went to a party in Providence and decided to park my car at a friend's house because I didn't want to drink and drive. A DUI was the last thing I needed. (I still had *some* wits about me.) My friend lived in a neighborhood that had a reputation for some crime, so I made sure to park in his driveway. I locked my car. I was confident that it would be OK. The car was the last thing of any value that I owned, a value that went far beyond what it was worth monetarily.

I woke up the next morning hungover and walked to my friend's house to get the car . . . and, well, to this day, I can conjure the feeling I had when I realized it wasn't there. I was totally hollowed out, mentally and physically. It was just a car, but it meant so much more to me. It was a symbol of one of the few things I had done right in my life—graduating from high school and getting into college. More than that, it was a symbol of the one time in my life when I had seemed to make my dad proud of me. And I had fucked it all up.

I was already in a bad place before the car was stolen. And now, I was knocked down even further. It was a big moment in my life. It felt like rock bottom, though I didn't know at the time that I still had a little ways to go to reach my lowest.

I contacted the cops, but they didn't offer much hope. Cars stolen in that neighborhood rarely, if ever, resurfaced.

I called my parents to tell them what had happened. My mom responded with empathy, but her voice was drowned out by my dad's. He, predictably, flipped out. He walked right out of the house and got into his car and drove from Long Island to Providence to pick me up.

When I got in the car with him, I decided to fess up to everything. I told him that I had dropped out of college months earlier. I kind of wanted him to yell, wanted it all to feel familiar. But I got nothing. Just four hours of that recognizable silence on the way home. It was the longest car ride of my life. But the silence this time was different from the silence when I returned home from military school. It wasn't just stubborn. It was dark and cold and angry. (By the way, to this day I wish I had finished college. I now hate leaving tasks uncompleted. I also feel like I failed my mom by not getting a college degree. But I don't let myself get buried by that regret. I use it as motivation for never failing at anything like that again. That pain has become a source of power.)

And, in the blink of an eye, I was back to square one. Back in my parents' house in East Hampton. Back to a life that had nothing to look forward to. A life that had nothing to look back on, no firewall of positivity to draw strength from or feel proud of. I really started to wonder again if anyone would miss me if I were gone, if they'd all just be better off without me around.

The breaking point—the moment when everything would change for me and my life—came just a week later.

• • •

At 4:00 A.M. on Thanksgiving Day, my dad walked into my room, shook me, and told me to get up, that we were going to Providence to get the rest of my stuff, which was in a storage unit.

"I'm not going," I told him, without getting out of bed. I just couldn't take his anger and disappointment. Not anymore. It wasn't that it would hurt me. It was that I had fallen into a place where I didn't feel *anything*, so it didn't matter. Nothing did.

My response stopped him cold for a moment. He looked surprised. But that look quickly disappeared from his face and was replaced by one of fury. He ordered me again to get up.

"I'm not going," I said.

He left my room. He woke up Phil instead, and the two of them headed up to Providence, where they packed up all of my stuff and drove back, arriving home around 4:00 P.M.

My dad walked through the door and right up to me and demanded I give him the keys to his Mitsubishi Montero, which I'd borrowed a few times in the last week (he'd charged me $25 a day to use it). I handed them over, but then I issued my own demand: I asked him for the money he owed me. I'd gotten something fixed on the Montero and had spent the last of my money—$1,500—doing so.

He charged out of the house and drove the Montero to an ATM. My mom begged me to not take the money from him when he returned. She, unlike my dad, had never given up on me. She knew I still had the ability and the time to turn things around. I didn't know that, though. Phil also begged me to not take the money. They both knew what doing so would signify. What they didn't know is that I no longer cared what happened to me.

When my dad walked back into the house, he held up the money in his fist.

"If you take this money," he said, his voice trembling with anger, "your life will forever change."

I snatched the money right out of his hand. He stared at me with raw hatred.

"You motherfucking piece of shit," he spat at me. "You'll never be shit in your life. Get the fuck out of this house."

That was it, I thought. *He said it. He finally told the truth about how he felt about me, about how he had always felt about me.* I no longer had to guess.

That realization got to me. It shook me out of the fog of indifference, reaching something within me that I thought no longer existed.

I walked out of the house. It was November 2012. And just like that, I never lived there again.

I called Jerome. He came and picked me up. I spent the next six months living with him, sleeping on the floor of his bedroom.

Suddenly, I *would* feel things again. But all I felt was pain. It hurt like nothing else ever had.

I realized that all of those times that I thought I had hit rock bottom before—getting kicked out of schools, getting sent to military school, getting my car stolen—had been mirages. I was there now, though. *This* is what it felt like. For the first time in my life, I had nothing to fall back on.

My dad was right. My decision to take the money *would* change my life. Forever.

He was just wrong about how that change would manifest itself.

• • •

At this point, the negativity in my life had been built up and had grown so heavy that I could no longer carry it. What my dad had said to me was the proverbial last straw.

But the real pain I felt from it also shook me out of the stupor that I'd been in all of my life.

I remember a moment I had within the first two weeks of

staying at Jerome's. It was three or four in the morning and I was lying on my makeshift bed on his floor. The house—and the world—was quiet, but my brain was buzzing. I stared at the ceiling and, for the first time in my life, asked myself: *What am I doing? Why am I living like this?*

All of that negativity in my life, that vicious circle that I'd been constantly caught in, was doing nothing for me. Most of the time, I had been doing as little as I could, just getting by, always hiding in plain sight. Other times, I had been going in reverse. I realized then that I had to *stop existing and start living.*

I hadn't been applying myself and I hadn't been present with myself. I'd been looking to others to validate my existence. I'd been letting my pain control me as opposed to turning it into my power.

I was not the author of my own story.

So much of "living" is about not letting opportunities for learning and growth pass us by, and for failing to engage in the world. We all learn and absorb things every single day—we do it when we listen, when we analyze and process. But if we're existing and not living, we will fail to recognize those things and fail to put them into practice. We fail to walk that bridge of gratitude, fail to realize that we have a ton to be grateful for. We fail to see and feel the love that exists all around us. We fail to see and appreciate the beauty that's all around us—the leaves on the trees, the blue in the sky, the smiles on the faces of strangers.

Merely existing narrows our vision. Living builds confidence and opens our eyes, giving us the ability to see all of the gratitude and love around us. And when we find that gratitude and love, we turn on our internal high beams, which allows us to glow. And light attracts light.

Remove the impediments to learning and absorbing. Stop worrying. Reflect and then move on. Dream about the future, but also focus on the moment at hand.

In the dark of that early morning on Jerome's floor, I decided that despite how painful rock bottom was, it did offer something, and this is important.

Rock bottom offers a choice.

I could sit still and remain in my misery. Or I could take a step—no matter how small—to try to get off the ground. I could finally, truly, start to apply myself.

With nothing really left to lose, I decided on the latter. What got me there is something else I thought about that night on Jerome's floor: how thankful I was for him and his family. They had shown me love with no strings attached. They didn't have to—they could have asked me to leave at any time. But they didn't. It blew my mind. And it made me realize that I had to do something in return. I owed something to them—and myself.

I had to prove my dad wrong. *He may be right about me now,* I thought. *But I swear, I will make him eat those words.* And the fog that had shrouded me all of my life started to lift.

CHAPTER 5

OUTWORK

There's a saying I came up with that I use all of the time in my classes: *We're not here to work, we're here to outwork.*

The idea is that we didn't come to wherever we are—a spin class, this book, our lives—just to work. Everybody "works." "Working" is just existing. "Outworking" is living.

It applies to any given task—the dishes, a presentation at work, a workout. How we do *anything* is how we do *everything*. It's one thing to go through the motions and complete the task. It's an entirely different level when you outwork it.

I see it sometimes when I teach a class. There are some participants who ride without a ton of effort. They finish the ride, yes, just like everyone else. But there are others who truly go for it during the ride, apply themselves, outwork it. It's obvious which group gets the most out of it. When I do my own exercising, I don't call it a "workout." I call it an "outwork," which helps me get in the right mindset.

This concept came to me, of course, from my mom. She never just worked. Outworking is how she taught herself a new language in a new country, why she did her hair and dressed up nicely to do errands, and how she became not only a teacher, but also an administrator. Outworking is her ethic.

My life started to change when it became mine.

• • •

The first step on my new journey was a rather practical one: I needed a job. That $1,500 I got from my dad was not going to last very long.

I took a few odd jobs here and there that tided me over for a month or two. And then one day toward the end of that winter, I got a call at Jerome's house. It was Jayvee, who used to come with, and sometimes without, Jerome to pick me up and drive me around when I needed to get out of my house in high school. She and Jerome were no longer dating but had remained good friends.

Jayvee was working for Flywheel, a new company that offered spin classes. She managed the company's studio location in East Hampton. She needed a maintenance staff going into the spring and summer. She knew I had been looking for a job and wondered if I would be interested.

I was twenty years old and was being offered a job as a janitor. "Hell, yes," I replied.

The job wasn't easy. My six-hour shift started at 6:30 A.M. Many days, I'd come back for another shift later in the afternoon. I didn't have a car anymore, so I sometimes borrowed Jerome's sister's moped to get there. If the moped wasn't available, I had to take a taxi.

My job consisted of mopping the floors, cleaning the toilets, and wiping down sweaty bikes. I wore rubber gloves all day, which made my hands clammy and pruned. Tuesdays were water delivery days, and well, it's still hard for me to believe just how much water Flywheel customers could drink. A truck delivered the water bottles on pallets. It took me and a few other guys three hours to bring them all inside.

The space at the East Hampton Flywheel was small and tight. The interior was all black, giving it a hip New York City–club vibe. There was an entry room with a counter, and a door with a little circular window, like you find on a ship, that led to the class space. Within that room were fifty stationary bikes lined up in rows, all facing the instructor's bike in the front, which was positioned to face out toward the room. Downstairs in the basement was a room known as Flybarre, where the barre and Pilates classes took place.

So, yes, I was a janitor. But it was steady work, steady as anything I'd ever done. And even though I knew I didn't want to be a janitor all of my life, I decided that it was an opportunity, one that I was not going to screw up. I mopped those floors and cleaned those toilets with intent and purpose. I channeled the lesson that my mom had provided to me by example: I outworked my job description. My mindset was that this wasn't a job that was "beneath" me. Sometimes we all have to humble ourselves in order to propel ourselves forward. Mopping floors helped me understand who I was. I never looked at it as a "less-than" job, but as one that I would do with a purpose. There is no job beneath us if we outwork it.

Flywheel was a new environment for me, like nowhere I had

ever been—a high-end fitness boutique with a bunch of rich and fancy people, and even a few celebrities, coming in and out of the place every day. I realized that people could "see" me, despite the differences in our socioeconomics and, for the most part, the color of our skin. I was right there in front of them. Instead of just trying to hide in plain sight, as I had done before, I decided to do something different. It didn't matter that I was *just* a janitor. Along with doing my best at cleaning, I also decided that part of outworking my job description would be how I expressed myself outwardly. I made sure I had a smile on my face at all times, and I greeted people with that smile and a hearty "hello" when customers came in the door. I felt like part of the Flywheel team, and I wanted to contribute to the place's welcoming vibe.

After a few weeks, I started to recognize some of the regular clients. I took notice of which spots they preferred in the studio so that when I saw them coming in from the parking lot, I'd rush in and clean and set up their bikes before they came in.

And, after those few weeks, a weird thing happened, at least something that was weird to me: I felt good. My job and the way I performed it made me feel confident. I started to feel gratitude for the job and the opportunity, and I woke up most days allowing myself to feel it. I stopped dwelling on my past and looked, for the first time, to some sort of future.

. . .

Outworking a job—and anything and everything in our lives—is really about maximizing our days and helping to create opportunity in our lives.

Applying that ethic to my first job at Flywheel helped unlock everything else in my life. I was hired as a janitor. It's not a dream job for many and it certainly wasn't for me. But I never sulked as I mopped and thought to myself that I was too good to be doing this, that I was above this kind of work. Nah. Instead, I mopped the shit out of those floors. I mopped them like I was the CEO. Those bikes had not a drop of sweat on them. Those toilets shined so bright they'd blind you. I smiled when I saw customers come in and engaged with them. I volunteered to do more work, to help out with whatever needed to be done. In outworking my job description, I was, in fact, auditioning for something better. At the time, I didn't know what that "better" was or when the opportunity might come. But I would be ready for it when it did.

• • •

For months, I did my shifts at Flywheel and then went back to Jerome's in the evenings. I was saving money for the first time in my life and feeling like there was a purpose in doing so. I had a future, I knew, though I had no idea what it would entail. I felt the motivation and confidence to apply for—and get—another job, this one at the Lululemon store in East Hampton. I worked the floor there, selling yoga pants. There was a crazy crossover in clientele between my two jobs—I sold $200 leggings in the afternoons at Lululemon to some of the same people whose bikes I had wiped down that morning.

I loved the vibe at Flywheel. Clients came there to work hard, to get in better shape. We, as a staff, worked just as hard. That work ethic, though, was coupled with a genuine feeling of friend-liness and inclusiveness, something that trickled down from the top. The cofounder and head honcho of Flywheel was a woman named Ruth Zukerman. She was also the lead instructor and the person who designed—and taught—the distinctive instruction method there.

Ruth had outworked her job description, too. When she had the idea for her first spin company, SoulCycle, there were some people who didn't take her seriously. She's a woman. Entrepre-neurs, especially at that time, were supposed to be bros who went to Stanford. But she didn't let that bias get in the way of her vision. She outworked what people thought she should be, her supposed station in life, the lane that she was supposed to stay in. And she went on to cofound SoulCycle and then Flywheel, two companies that pretty much reinvented the spin industry. She killed it.

And she killed it with kindness. One of the reasons that Ruth was so successful, I think, is because she is so cool and super-loving. She was one of those rare people you come across in life who looks at everyone equally and treats them that way, too. She treated me the same as she treated any celebrity who came to a Flywheel class. She was totally authentic. I even had a little crush on her. I once asked Jayvee to do a little reconnaissance for me and to run by Ruth the idea of me asking her out on a date. (See? I *was* starting to feel good, more confident.) Jayvee reported back three things: (1) Ruth was impressed by how ballsy I was, (2) she was flattered, especially because I was thirty years younger than she was, and (3) there was no way in hell that she would go out on a date with an employee. It had been worth the shot.

The weeks and months went by at Flywheel. And the longer I was there, the more I started to pay attention to the actual classes that were being taught. I listened to the music through the walls. As I was mopping the floors, I would stop moving around my yellow slop bucket for a moment when I got to the studio door, so I could peek through that circular window and watch what was going on. The instructors fascinated me. All of them were really good at Flywheel, but two of them really stuck out: Ruth and a woman named Holly Rilinger, who was a master instructor. They both seemed to be in total control, of themselves and of the class. When they pushed their riders, their riders responded. From the looks on the faces of the riders, you could actually see the transformation that took place in the class. Ruth and Holly instilled a sense of determination and confidence in the class. In doing so, they changed their riders' lives, if only for that moment or that day. The way that Ruth and Holly were able to motivate their riders to do things they didn't believe they could do before they walked into that class that morning seemed to me to be some sort of magic trick.

And at the same time, Ruth and Holly looked like they were having so much fun. They were sending out great vibes and then glowing with the positive feedback as those vibes were returned to them.

They were also playing some raw-ass music, some of the rap—Tupac, Biggie, Jay-Z—that I loved, with all of the cuss words and nothing bleeped out. I couldn't believe it. These two tiny, proper-looking white women doing some club-banging. They were so dope. The energy in the class was so pure.

Ruth used to allow me and my coworkers, Jared and John (who were also great friends of mine), to play our own music as we cleaned the bike studio after everyone was gone. As I cleaned I started to subconsciously count off the beats of the music—*one-two, one-two*—using some of the skills I'd learned in military school and in college. I looked at the instructor's bike, under the halo of lights, at the front of the class. And I started to dream a bit.

A few more weeks went by, Jared, John, and I continuing to clean the studio, playing our own music. And gradually I started to visualize myself doing something different at Flywheel, something other than mopping the floors.

• • •

John and I were putting away our mops one day after cleaning the bike studio when I turned to him.

"John, I think I can do this," I said, motioning around the room.

"Do what?"

"Teach classes."

"How you figure?"

I had been thinking a lot about how I "figure" it. I had learned about cadence and timing in military school while doing drills, while marching, while shouting out callbacks to the drill sergeants. I could vocalize—I had a naturally deep voice, but it had become more effective and commanding in military school. I had learned about counting music, about cues, and about sound design when I had studied the A/V stuff in college. The discipline of staying in good shape had been instilled in me since military school—I stayed in shape by playing basketball whenever I could. Exercising remains one of the few things in life that you are always happy afterward that you did.

I had, in a way, been preparing for this for much of my life. But I never knew it or understood it. Until now.

The one problem: I'd never taken a spin class and, in fact, had never been on a road bike or a stationary bike in my life. My experience with bikes had been riding Huffys around the neighborhood and popping wheelies with Jerome. But I felt something in my gut: I could do this.

I watched more classes through that little window. I watched the instructors, watched how they moved, how they led. I listened to what they said. I listened to the music. I started to actually prepare—to try. I "practiced" running a class with no bike. I put music on and sat in a chair and moved and spoke and instructed a class of imaginary riders in front of me.

I mentioned my idea to some coworkers at Lululemon. Pretty much all of them thought I was crazy to even think about it.

The typical response: "Bro, you trippin'. You've never even been on a bike."

But I knew I could do it. I believed it. I just needed to try.

One night when I was hanging out on Jerome's porch with him and Jared and John, I told them that I was going to ask Ruth in the next week if I could become an instructor. They thought I was joking at first, and they laughed. Then they looked at me and realized I was serious and stopped laughing.

"Man, go get it," Jerome said.

A few days later, I woke up one morning and felt it. I finally had worked up the courage I needed.

I went into work early that day. While I cleaned I kept an eye out of the window on the parking lot. I wanted to talk to Ruth privately so no one else would hear me.

I saw her car pull up. I went outside, carrying a bag of trash even though it was only a quarter full and didn't need to be taken out yet. Ruth got out of her car. I walked up to her.

"Ruth, I have kind of a random thing I wanted to talk to you about."

"Sure," she said with a smile. As always.

"I, um, think I can be an instructor. I think I can lead a class." Silence.

I had no idea what she was going to say to that. I thought she might laugh in my face or tell me that she'd pass along the idea to someone else—anything that would get her out of an awkward situation that she didn't want to be in. I was a janitor at a spin studio asking to be a spin instructor, after all. I thought that if she blew me off, well, at least I had finally worked up the courage to try something for real, to take myself outside of my comfort zone. There's a famous Wayne Gretzky quote that goes, "You miss 100 percent of the shots you don't take." If I failed, this was a failure I'd be OK with. I would learn something from it.

Instead, she stopped walking and looked me straight in the eye.

"Are you serious about this, Alex?"

"Yes, I am."

"OK. Give me two weeks of your time to train you, and I can change your life."

PART TWO

LOOK GOOD

CHAPTER 6

THE JOURNEY AND THE DESTINATION

Feeling good is the foundation for activating our greatness. Feeling good comes from waking up every day and expressing gratitude and being present with ourselves and preparing and trying. A purposeful shift in mindset. That shift comes when *instead of viewing ourselves as who we used to be, we view ourselves as who we want to be.*

This is important. We are all in control of the narratives we construct about ourselves. We *can* push away the negative, destructive thoughts when we find our gratitude, take time to be present with ourselves, prepare and really work through whatever is slowing us down. Doing all of that allows us to tell a new story. We become the heroes of our own futures, not the villains of our past failures. We do this by building the discipline, by taking all of these steps over and over again. That leads to increased self-confidence and awareness.

And . . . we start to feel good. And then a transformation

takes place. Feeling good leads directly to looking good. Now, what I mean by that is looking good *to ourselves*. In our purest form. It has nothing to do with our outside veneer, our clothes, our hair, our Instagram posts. There is no masking.

For my entire life up until I found the courage to talk to Ruth in the Flywheel parking lot, I had done all the things we deem necessary in our society to look good. I "looked good" when I went out at night to parties, to a club. I "looked good" when people posted pictures of me on social media. I wore nice clothes and had fresh sneakers. I kept my Caesar haircut clean and tight. During my teenage years, I finally ditched those nerdy glasses. And I had stayed in good physical shape since military school and had maintained a healthy diet.

But none of that mattered. Not the clothes, not the shape I was in. None of it could fix the self-doubt or provide the confidence that I was missing. All it did was mask my insecurities, to everyone else but me. When I stared into the mirror, I saw right through the new Ralph Lauren shirt and my fresh line-up. You can wear designer clothes and still look like a clown. Nothing we do on the outside means anything if we don't feel good about ourselves. Once we do that, we start to look in the mirror and embrace the person staring back at us. We give ourselves the grace to fail. But we also set goals and create a game plan.

In that mirror, we eventually see a champion.

We're finally living, not just existing. And that newfound energy and self-love damn sure looks good *on* us, too.

And when we feel good, we start to move differently, at a different frequency. We give off a different vibe. We start to exude that internal glow.

If we are wearing a nice outfit and someone says to us, "Hey, you look nice," that's a compliment. But when someone tells us that we have great energy, that we have a great vibe, that's a top-tier compliment. They see something projecting outward from inside. They see a glow.

And when we give off that glow, we do two things. First, we attract others with that same vibe. Second, our glow helps other people find their own glow. Energy is contagious.

Looking good is another big step up the mountain.

Now, we might think to ourselves that feeling good and looking good are luxuries, that we can't attain them because we have too many things going on in our lives, that we are not as fortunate as others. We might think that someone more fortunate than us has an easier time than all of us, that because of their status or money a CEO, a famous person, a rich person, can easily feel good and look good.

This could not be further from the truth. Everyone—regardless of status, money, or job—can feel good and look good. Think of some everyday interactions we have with other people. Think, maybe, of the grocery store. Think of the guy who bags your groceries and gives off the vibe that he would rather be anywhere else on the planet. Sullen. No eye contact. No interaction at all.

Then there's the other grocery bagger, the one who engages with you, who asks about your day, who smiles, who is present and attentive, who goes the extra mile to assist the patrons.

We are sometimes not even conscious of what happens during and after our interactions with other people, but the ripples caused by how we dive into life are always felt by others in the pool. The sullen guy brings us down with him. But the energetic one boosts us up. He gives off a great vibe. Rich in spirit. Nothing can stop him from looking good.

And guess what's coming right back at him?

But remember that this is all a process, and it's not a straight, linear one at that. It zigs and zags.

By the time I started my instructor training at Flywheel, I certainly felt good on the inside, but I wasn't all the way there. I still had my doubts. I was still nervous and anxious. I could still feel the demon of all of my failures and all of that negativity in my life right there behind me, salivating, waiting for me to slip up and succumb to those dark emotions. There were still mornings when I woke up on Jerome's floor and felt depressed. And that depression would sometimes lead to dark thoughts. There were days when I thought about giving it all up. There were days when I wondered if I deserved to feel good, that I was an imposter who would be outed at any time. Other times I was tempted to go out and party all night and blow off my job in the morning, something I got good at doing in college.

But all of those things were just thoughts. My actions held up. I wouldn't have been able to put it in these words back then, but my actions held up because I had taken the steps to feeling good about myself. The pain I felt from some of my past experiences used to overwhelm me. But I was now using it as motivation. Mainly because I had made it through them.

I had started to take some time for myself in the mornings to kind of do a rundown of how I felt. If I felt good—physically, emotionally, mentally—I ran with it. If I felt the breath of the demon—those old bad habits trying to claw their way back into my head—I tried to figure out why it was happening and then tried to think my way out of it.

I felt gratitude every day, not only for Jerome and his family, but also for Ruth and my job, and for the chance I had been blessed with to get things right.

I was growing in confidence in my own abilities through my actions. I was actually applying myself, and not just going through the motions in life. I was trying and preparing like I never had before in my life as I went through those training weeks. And when I screwed up—which I did—I didn't get down or let it rattle me. I used it as a learning opportunity.

I had a future. It was still a bit opaque. But I knew it was there, and I knew it would be different from and better than my past. I learned an important lesson about personal growth: Changing the way I viewed myself was everything.

I wasn't there yet. In fact, in the beginning at least, the progress I was making was sometimes painfully slow. But I was allowing myself to *feel* that progress, even though it wasn't as fast as I would have hoped or liked. And I think that's an important thing to keep in mind on our way up the mountain to activating our greatness. That *a slow progression is still progression*.

Everyone wants it all right away. But life doesn't work that way, of course. Sometimes we work very hard at something and have very little to show for it. Sometimes we even take a step backward.

Progress can be a funny, tricky thing. Most often, it comes in drops, not in buckets. The arc of progress is often painfully slow, so slow that many people mistake it for a lack of progress. All that matters is that you don't quit. That opportunity might be right around the corner.

There are no shortcuts when it comes to changing our lives, to overcoming negativity, feeling good, looking good, and doing better. Overcoming setbacks and roadblocks is the point. "If there is no struggle, there is no progress," Frederick Douglass once said. The key is to make the struggles work *for* us and not *against* us.

One way to do that is to train ourselves for real-life resistance. We do this by practicing it. In a workout, we can push ourselves to run or bike that extra mile. At home, when we want to understand something more fully, we can put away the phone and turn off the TV and sit down and read about it, with our full attention. We can outwork our job description so that when that promotion comes, we are fully ready.

In my classes, we manufacture the struggle, we force resistance. When I feel like the class is coasting a bit, I'll look into the camera and say: ***If it's too light, turn that shit to the right***. (Turning the resistance knob on the bike to the right makes it more difficult.) The "resistance" we turn up in class is a proxy for the setbacks, the potholes, and the negativity we come across in real life. When we do it in class at game speed, it teaches and trains and helps us to overcome it when it shows up outside of class. We can do this in our own lives by getting out of our comfort zone, by accepting a new challenge. Put your name in for that big job. Take up a new hobby that you know nothing about. Learn a new language.

Whatever we do, we can't be scared to fail. When we're working out, resistance is what breaks down our muscles, which ultimately leads to them getting stronger. This voluntarily added-on resistance makes us stronger mentally. We train our minds to be patient, resilient, and committed, and to not give up. If we train ourselves enough in this way, we start to embrace the resistance and run toward it rather than shy away from it. This is another example of living and not merely existing. We start to turn it into our power.

And we'll need this on those days, weeks, or even months when we have little or nothing to show for our hard work toward progress. Because when that happens, it's easy to feel down or even feel like giving up.

For me, there was progress unseen as I mopped the floors at Flywheel. I just kept going, doing the best I could every single day I was there. I had no idea what, if anything, would come out of going about it that way. But I knew that there was a better chance of something good happening if I prepared, tried, and executed. I was pretty certain that *nothing* would come from it if I didn't give it my best. I'd been down that road before, many times.

If we keep trying, preparing, and pushing ourselves forward and being OK with—and learning from—failures, progress *will* happen, even if it happens slower than we like. Eventually, there will come a time when we *will* see it and feel it and know it's happening. And our success in achieving it will be that much sweeter for having overcome the resistance.

One way to think about slow progress—a way to make it easier to digest—is to rethink this rather tired cliché:

"Life is about the journey, not the destination."

We all try to live by this axiom. It is a way of making the world more manageable by taking everything step-by-step and not worrying about the big, imposing end goal. It's a way of enjoying the ride along the way and learning to love the process and the struggle. There's a reason that this day-by-day thinking is such a big part of substance abuse recovery programs—it's an ideal way to view our lives.

But, man, it's very hard to live our lives in the way that this adage dictates. We're human. We want to fast-forward to the good parts. We want to win the lottery, lose ten pounds in a week, take a pill to make us instantly happier, get rid of the resistance. We all know, intuitively, that it's about the journey, the grind, but we can't seem to embrace it in the moment as we're told we should. This saying is much easier to live up to after we've reached the desired destination.

I thought about this axiom and why it might not work as well as it should in real time, while we're on the journey. I came up with a remix to it, a way to rethink it that, I believe, can make it more practical and useful for us.

So, yes, we do actually have to take the steps, start small, focus on the little things before us, and fall in love with the journey and all it encompasses. But I think we must also acknowledge that the journey isn't everything. That's right. The axiom instructs us to concentrate solely on the journey and not pay any mind to the destination. But I don't think that's the way to get the most out of it. The destination shouldn't just be ignored. It is important and should be paid attention to, because it is what gives our journey its shape, its reason for being. So, in that way, we must embrace and fall in love with the journey, but we also must embrace and fall in love with the destination, as well.

Athletes like LeBron James and musicians like Jay-Z talk about "the process" all the time, about how the key to success, much less a good fulfilling life, is concentrating on, and falling in love with, the process, which is another word for the journey. This is all very true, of course.

What these people don't say out loud, though, is implied: We must also fall in love with the idea of the destination. The destination is the reason we are on the journey in the first place. It validates the existence of our chosen path.

What's also important to understand is that the destination is not some final endpoint. We don't just stop when we get there. Instead, we use it as a launching point for our next journey. It becomes part of that process.

This type of thinking is critical when it comes to feeling good, looking good, and doing better. Feeling good and looking good are part of the journey. Doing better is the destination, the reason why we are on the journey. But doing better, because it is not about the self but about others, is just the starting point for another journey with a new destination.

The journey and the destination continuously regenerate, like flowers and love. It's a virtuous cycle that gives our lives movement over the terrain we travel, which is always changing—it will be different on Monday than how it is on Friday. It gives our lives meaning—we fall in love with the journey and the destination because we are living and not existing. And, in the end, our path rewards us with greatness.

• • •

Ruth had asked for two weeks of my time to train me as an instructor. I gave them to her with my undivided attention.

At the time, all Flywheel instructor training took place at the company's headquarters, which was located in the Flatiron District of Manhattan, a two and a half hour commute each way from East Hampton. Luckily for me, a friend of mine, Grace Fryman—who worked as a member liaison at Flywheel—offered me a couch in her apartment on the Upper West Side. I took her up on it. Moving from the floor to a couch felt like some sort of progress.

Every day for those two weeks I got on the subway near Grace's apartment and rode twenty minutes downtown to the Flatiron District for the training classes. I gave those classes everything I had, partially because I knew this was my chance and partially because I was a bit of an outcast there: All of the other instructors in the training program had a fitness or dance background. I had come from mopping floors.

At the end of the two weeks, I had my audition, which consisted of a seven-minute ride during which I instructed Ruth; Kate Hickl, an instructor who was already becoming a legend in the spin world; and Alison Cohen, another budding legend who was a master instructor.

I had known, of course, about the audition and I had been thinking about it and planning for it and working on it since the beginning of my training. I had decided to use two songs from Jay-Z's *Magna Carta Holy Grail*, an album that had changed my life. It was influenced by Jay-Z's painful relationship with his father and was all about breaking through the establishment. I chose the song "BBC"—with its refrain, "Let's work"—for the first part of the ride. And I chose the song "Crown," in which Jay-Z declares himself the king of hip-hop, to get into the proper frame of mind for the more difficult second part of the ride. I spent hours getting down the timing of the songs and thinking about what I would say and how I would motivate. When the day of the audition arrived, I knew I was prepared.

When I entered the Flatiron studio, I was nervous, but the nervousness helped me lock in. It was in the afternoon, in between the lunchtime and after-work classes. Ruth, Kate, and Alison hopped on their bikes. All of the lights were off, save for the spotlight on me. In my mind, I pictured an entire class in front of me. I took a deep breath and then ripped through the workout to the two songs.

When I was done, I felt great. Ruth turned on the studio lights. She and Kate and Alison huddled together, whispering, and every once in a while they would shoot concerned looks my way. *Oh shit*, I thought for a moment. *What's happening here?*

And then they all turned to me, and Ruth said: "We're just messing with you, Alex."

She and Alison were smiling. Ruth turned to Kate.

"Wow," was all she said.

Ruth then told me: "It's your time."

And I was off.

• • •

I was the youngest instructor on the Flywheel team. (Though being the youngest at military school was a horrible experience, I was excited about this one.) I was one of the few Black instructors.

Ruth told me that I could bring something to spin that had never been witnessed before. She didn't explain exactly what she meant when she said that, but looking back, I think I understand. There were no straight, young Black males in the spin industry back then. So that differentiated me. But so did my background: immigrant family, military school, growing up in East Hampton. I had so many different facets of life to tap into and an understanding of many different demographics. I brought a different sauce, that's for sure.

I took her saying that as both a validation and an invitation to be myself and push it all as far as I could take it. At the age of twenty, I had finally found something meaningful in my life.

In retrospect, the timing of all of this was really fortuitous, ripe for someone like me to enter the industry as an instructor. Spin classes were in their ascendance at the time, absolutely beginning to boom, offering a glimpse of the heights they would eventually achieve. They had an incredible buzz.

Much of that growth and hipness was due to Ruth. She'd been at the forefront of the craze. In 2006, she'd cofounded SoulCycle, a studio spin class that was the first big player in the space. Four years later, after she had left SoulCycle, she cofounded Flywheel, which helped propel the craze to an entirely new altitude.

Ruth was a visionary. She'd tapped into some unrecognized desire that people had to do spin workouts together, in a communal way, led by an instructor. What made it visionary is that it flew in the face of conventional wisdom at the time. Yes, there had been an aerobics-class craze a few decades before. But, at the time, the general vibe was that people like to work out on their own. Nike and Under Armour were airing TV ads of people doing solo workouts and going for runs by themselves on gritty city streets. But Ruth identified something that was bubbling under the surface. After she started the craze with SoulCycle, others had jumped in. Barre, yoga, and CrossFit classes had begun to grow, as well. But spin was royalty. And Ruth was its queen. Celebrities like Beyoncé, Michelle Obama, and Bradley Cooper were not only taking spin classes, but they were also talking about them in public. In cities—first in New York and Los Angeles, and then all over the country—people were clamoring to pay thirty-five dollars for a forty-five-minute class (the only length of class offered in those early days). The classes became can't-miss events, and sold out within minutes of being posted online. People showed up thirty minutes early for some classes just to claim a bike in the front row. Ruth always trained and preached that instructors were secondary to the classes. Her mantra was that the stars of the classes were the riders, and that's where the focus should be. Despite that, some of the best instructors started to develop dedicated followings.

Ruth's vision and execution with SoulCycle and Flywheel would pave the way for the next iteration of spin classes, the at-home, livestreamed version that would play a huge role in my life. In a significant way, she helped make Peloton—and me—possible.

. . .

After my training, I went back out to East Hampton (and Jerome's floor). And then came the day of my first class. . . .

I climbed up into the saddle of the bike, locked my feet into the pedals, took a deep breath, and looked out over the crowd in the East Hampton Flywheel studio. I couldn't see all that well—a bright light was trained on me while the rest of the room was dark—but I could tell that the room was filled to capacity, that every bike had a rider. My first class. Sold out. Fifty people had signed up for a class with me, a totally unproven entity as an instructor. They were here because of Ruth's faith in me, because of the trust they had in her and in Flywheel. They were here, too, because they had witnessed me, day after day, mopping the floors, cleaning off the bikes, with integrity and purpose.

I had prepared my ass off for this class. I made a playlist and had it memorized, backward and forward. I was going to start with Brass Knuckles's "Water Gun" remix that featured John Ryan. I threw in an up-tempo remix of Whitney Houston's "I Wanna Dance with Somebody" because it's a fun-ass song. I had practiced the class on the bike in the studio late at night when everyone else was gone. I had run through the cues and the warm-up, the climbs, the breaks, the intervals, and the cooldown. I had the timing of everything down cold.

And yet, I was still nervous as hell. Sweat had already started to drip off my face and onto the monitor between my bike handles, blurring the displayed numbers and words.

Fifty people. There were some regulars, people whose bikes I had prepared and cleaned for the last year. Ruth and some of my fellow instructors were out there. So were some friends from town. They were all there, waiting for me to start the class and to move them, in more ways than one.

I hit the cue for "Water Gun," and those first techno beats popped through the speakers. I took one more deep breath. I remembered to erase any potential signs of nervousness from my face with a big smile. I pulled the mini-microphone down over my mouth. And then, in my best military school voice, I said, loud and clear—and maybe a bit too fast:

"My name is Alex Toussaint."

I started to pedal and bob my head up and down with the beat of the music. I looked out over the studio and saw a blur of legs starting to move, to pedal.

"I'll be your instructor here today. Thank you from the bottom of my heart for showing up . . ." A beat passed. "Now let's show out!"

I turned up the music, and away we went.

Forty-five minutes later. The music stopped. Sweat was pouring off me, a good bit of it pooled under my bike. I was in a zone, caught up in my head, like no one else was around, just me and my thoughts. Surreal. I snapped back into the present when I heard the claps, the *whoop*s. I unclipped my feet from the pedals and we all—the entire class and me—walked outside of the building and into the sunshine. It was a tradition at Flywheel after a new instructor does his or her first class, this greeting, this celebration. Handshakes. High fives. Sweaty hugs. Ruth standing to the side, beaming.

The crowd eventually started to break up, people getting into their cars and going about the rest of their day. I walked back inside the studio and opened up the closet. I was still buzzing. I had some trouble pulling the yellow gloves over my sweaty hands. I grabbed a bottle of disinfectant and a rag. And then I began to wipe down the bikes, starting with the one I had just been on, and then working the rows, from left to right. I couldn't help but smile as I cleaned.

I was now officially an instructor.

I was also still a janitor.

· · ·

Some of my clients seemed to *see* me for the first time when I became an instructor. People who had never batted an eye in my direction were suddenly like, "Oh my God, look at you!" I never let that get me down. Some people in this world just don't talk to "the help." That's just life. I could have held a grudge, I guess, but instead I just decided to be grateful that they acknowledged me at all. That was a win. But still, to this day, I do what I always have: I try to treat everybody, regardless of their station in life, with the same level of respect. In other words, I treat people the same way Ruth treated me.

I led another class. And then another. And then another after that. My confidence was growing with each one. I was improving, tweaking things, learning from my mistakes (talking too fast, pushing too hard, etc.).

Ruth came to me one day. "You know you can quit the janitor job now and just concentrate on instructing full-time, if you want."

I told her I appreciated that, but I wanted to hold on to my other job, too, for the time being. Yes, the extra money from that job was nice. (By this time, I was no longer working at Lululemon.) But I still wanted to do it and felt like I *needed* to do it. I was getting a lot of positive feedback on the bike. But being a janitor kept me from getting a big head.

It also fed that chip on my shoulder. I needed to prove that I could outwork. To my dad. And to myself.

So, for my first two months of instructing at Flywheel, I would go in early to work, clock in, and then mop the floors and clean the bathrooms. Then I'd clock out, get into my biking outfit, clock back in, and teach a class. After the class, I'd get off the bike and say goodbye to the riders as they slowly made their way out of the studio. As soon as the last person left, I'd go clock out, clock back in, and then start wiping down the bikes. Not too long after I finished with the bikes, the people in the next class would start trickling into the studio. Same process. Instruct and then clean. For those two months, I worked about eighty hours a week.

I started off teaching just a few classes a week, but that number quickly grew. After a few weeks of instructing, I was doing fifteen classes a week, which was the maximum for Flywheel instructors. I felt like I was physically and mentally ready to do more. In a weird way, I may have been channeling my dad in order to best him, trying to fill my days with so much to stay ahead of something. Maybe my past.

I asked Ruth if I could add more classes.

"Why?" she asked.

Because I have something to prove, I thought. I didn't say that, though. I just told her I wanted more work and felt ready for it.

"I can't get you that many classes out here," she said. "You'll have to travel and instruct in the city. You OK with that?"

I was.

Ruth gave me an additional ten classes. I finally had to drop the janitor job. But I didn't lack for work. My weekly schedule now looked like this:

Mondays and Wednesdays: Teach a 9:30 and 10:30 class in East Hampton. Quick lunch and then take a Jitney bus to the city. Take the subway to the Upper East Side and teach a 4:30 class. Take the subway down to the Flatiron studio and teach a 7:30 and an 8:30 class there. Stay on Grace's couch.

Tuesdays and Thursdays: Teach three classes a day at various studios around the city. Take a Jitney back out to East Hampton on Thursday night.

Fridays, Saturdays, and Sundays: In East Hampton, teach three classes a day.

My motto back then was "No days off," and I lived up to it.

(Let me just get this straight here: Back then, I did everything wrong, at least when it came to taking care of myself physically. I didn't get enough sleep. I ate at McDonald's. I didn't stretch. I was not smart about any of it, but I was able to pull it off because I was a young dude with fresh legs. It wasn't until later, with my next step, that I realized that this was a career and not just a job. I needed to take care of myself by working out, sleeping well, and eating better, and I started to do just that.)

In order to help me stay motivated, I came up with an idea that helped get me in the right mindset for every week of work: *Don't chase Friday on Monday.*

Monday gets a bad rap. A lot of us wake up on that day with a sense of dread about the week ahead, about the work, about the long days. We look forward to Friday, to the feeling of relief that comes when the freedom of a weekend is upon us.

But that's wasteful thinking. And "thinking" is all it is. It's about our mindset, which is up to us to change and program.

Friday is the destination, yes. Let it shape our weekly journey. But learn to love and embrace the path, as well. The idea is to train your mind to get excited for the opportunity that Monday morning brings, for the opportunity to get back to work. The weekends (or any days off) are about chilling out and recharging our minds, bodies, and souls. Feeling dread on Monday only negates that recharging. Finding our gratitude, being present and prepared, and realizing we are progressing no matter how slow we feel on Monday morning can get us going in the right direction with the right mindset.

At that time at Flywheel, I was loving my work. But there were still days when I had to dig down deep to make it all happen. Resetting my mindset on Monday morning helped with that. My Monday classes are now my favorite ones of the week. They're where it all starts. We don't come to Monday to survive the week. We come to *thrive* the week.

CHAPTER 7

DISCIPLINE OVER DISTRACTIONS

When we first start to feel good and look good, we (paradoxically) enter a precarious zone. After we break away from the negativity for the first time and have taken those first steps up the mountain, we can get reckless. It's a little bit of "relief syndrome," where we can take our eye off the ball for a bit. And if we aren't careful, this is the moment we can slip and send ourselves tumbling back down.

Here is where we have to rely on the foundation that we've built, when we have to *maintain discipline over distractions*.

Despite the fact that I was far too young at military school for it to be a positive experience while I was there, I have mad respect for the military. I want to get that straight. My dad served, of course, but so did his brother, Uncle Ronald, who was a master sergeant in the air force and the first person of Haitian descent to serve on Air Force One (during the Clinton presidency). And, as painful as military school was at the time I was going through it, the lessons I learned there were beginning to bear real fruit.

Military school is, of course, where I learned a lot about discipline. While I did a lot of marching on the quad—which required discipline—I also did a lot of standing at attention. Utterly still, holding my rifle, staring straight ahead. And while I did this, drill sergeants made it their job to try to make me falter, to break my discipline with distractions. They'd drop things behind me that made a loud noise, try to make me flinch. They yelled cuss words in my face, spitting all over me in the process. If I moved at all—even a hard blink—I'd get smoked and I'd get sticks.

Discipline is at the heart of military training. You're being prepared, in essence, to be able to execute your commands flawlessly at game speed so that you'll be ready in even the most chaotic environments (like a war zone). Your discipline is what allows you to keep going through distractions, even major ones. It is a conditioned behavior, a mindset that becomes muscle memory.

For most of us, our discipline—that foundation—is conditioned by our everyday behaviors. By being present with ourselves and through our preparation, we make it possible to embrace the steps we make on the journey and the destination. It includes finding and maintaining our inner light and being aware of our energy and vibe and allowing it to shine for ourselves and others. When we have that foundation of discipline, no one and no thing can knock us off that track. Nothing can break our perspective. It's the muscle memory that allows us to get the task at hand done and done well.

Distractions are everywhere. Our distractions are someone telling us we can't reach our goals. Negativity is a distraction. Distractions are little voices of doubt in our heads. Distractions are wasting time, or allowing stress and anxiety to overcome us. They can surface as anything in our lives that can knock us off our track.

At this time in my life, distractions came in many forms. It was that little voice telling me to stay out later than I should. It was the other voice telling me, *hey, you're doing great, they love you, it won't matter if you don't give it your all during class today*. It was that demon of my past failures lurking over my shoulder.

Distractions are the lack of motivation to do what we know we should. And discipline is what allows us to overcome these distractions. Because ***our discipline will carry us when motivation won't***.

Some mornings, even now, I wake up and I'm just not motivated. Maybe I have a cold. Or maybe I had a falling-out with a good friend the night before. Whatever the reason, sometimes I wake up and it just isn't there. We all have times like that. There are 365 days in a year (and one more than that every four years). It's impossible to wake up on each of those days and be motivated. We all go through a lot of shit in life.

But when I lack motivation, I still have my discipline—which I've worked to strengthen for moments just like this—to fall back on. When we are not motivated, it's like the electricity has gone out. In that moment, discipline becomes our backup generator. Discipline helps us not chase Fridays. It's what keeps us mentally and physically fit. This fitness that discipline instills in us means that when something bad does happen—and it will—we have something to lean on to help push us.

So how do we get that discipline? It starts with the smallest things.

. . .

The first thing we should acknowledge is that we are already disciplined in a lot of the facets of our lives. I say this to you moms and dads out there—if you have kids, you do all you can to help them succeed, right? That's discipline. If we have coworkers who rely on us, we have discipline. And don't forget who relies on us the most: We are accountable for ourselves. Discipline is about responsibility.

Discipline is also about how we condition our minds. I'll give you an example. I told you about how I "outwork" basically six days a week, with running and lifting weights. By now, I know exactly what I get out of it, the good it does for my body and mind. I've experienced those blue skies. So, when the inevitable happens, and the day dawns cloudy (figuratively or literally), and I just don't have any juice or motivation, I think about those blue skies. I know that if I get up off my butt and run or lift, those clouds will part. When we seek motivation, it becomes, in itself, a form of discipline.

Being disciplined doesn't mean we have to be some rigid, uptight person, always grinding. No way. Fun is a big part of life. I would argue that being disciplined enhances the fun portion of our lives, and we have to be disciplined, too, about finding time to blow off steam and laugh and chill out.

There are plenty of other ways to instill discipline on our lives.

Here's another instance where my experience in military school has helped me later in life. Remember how I had to make my bed perfectly every morning, with those hospital corners and tight sheets? I didn't understand why we had to do it back then. It seemed kind of pointless, to be honest. We were just going to get right back into bed that night. But I get it now. In his famous graduation speech at the University of Texas, Admiral William H. McRaven—the guy who commanded the Navy SEAL mission that got Osama bin Laden—talked about his military training and, in particular, about being forced to make his bed perfectly every morning. That one simple task, when completed well, he said, leads to every other task throughout your day being completed well. Remember: How we do *anything* is how we do *everything*. As McRaven said in his speech: "If you want to change the world, start off by making your bed."

That's what discipline is.

So, I make my bed every morning and do a kick-ass job at it and everything else flows from there. I count my blessings. I shout in the mirror. I take a moment to be present with myself. I acknowledge my emotions and what's going on with me. All of these things are part of my discipline.

Discipline, too, is about preparation. If we're trying to get to the gym in the morning before work, it's a good idea to get our gym clothes ready and put our sneakers by the door the night before. We prepare so that we put ourselves in the position—and give ourselves a little extra room—to win.

Discipline is how we react when things don't go as planned. If we work on it enough—and avoid distractions—it becomes our baseline and part of our character.

Purpose is also our discipline. I have a close friend, Jeff Blue, who also went to a military school. He is a motivated, get-things-done kind of guy. One day he was talking to me about how he strove to live his life, and it caught my attention. "On purpose, with purpose," is what he said.

I liked that saying a lot. I thought about it for a while, and then I remixed it a bit and came up with this: *Move with purpose, execute with intention*. It is a great way to work on our discipline. In a bigger sense, it is the way we should proceed through our daily lives.

Moving with a purpose and executing with intention is about not *whatever-ing* our day away. It's about not only having direction, understanding our journey and where we are on that journey, and appreciating the goals that give that journey shape, but also recognizing that those goals cannot be chased without thought, planning, and execution. We need to nail down our purpose and then move, with our full hearts and minds, thinking about the steps we are taking and thinking about where those steps are taking us. In other words, executing with intent.

Think about serious golfers and tennis players. When they practice, they don't just thoughtlessly and casually hit the ball. Every practice swing they make has a reason—or a purpose—behind it. Every swing is made with intent.

It's the same thing in a Peloton class. Sure, you could just hop on the bike and half-ass it. No one is watching but you. But in order to get something out of the class, you have to do it with purpose and intent. Every class is an audition for life, just as every practice swing for a golfer or tennis player is an audition for a real match.

All of this ties into living, not just existing. Existing is allowing a stationary bike to remain stationary. Living is realizing that the bike can take you places. It ties into the preparation we need to make, as well. Having a purpose and executing it with intention require being prepared to do so.

"Move with purpose, execute with intention" goes for really anything and everything in life. Our families, our jobs, what we do in our communities. Any little task we undertake (like making our beds) should be done this way. It's about the whole self, about following through and about sustained progress. It's about not overindulging on things that make us feel bad, whether that's alcohol or social media. We can't go to the gym, work hard, and then go home and eat crappy food. We can't do a great job at work and then come home and get wasted. Move with a purpose at the gym and at work and during your days. And then execute with intention when we get home.

So how can we help activate that discipline, purpose, and intention every day?

One way to do it is to start with a playlist.

Music, as you can tell, has always been a huge part of my life. It is the language I use to communicate and connect with my emotions. It makes me *feel*.

Music is, of course, a massive part of spin classes. (Imagine doing a class without it?) In class, it's the music that connects our bodies and minds. It makes us move *and* it makes us think. Kendrick Lamar's "Let Me Be Me" is all about dealing with external pressures and doing what it takes to be true to oneself. Drake's "Nice for What" talks about living a real life and not a virtual one through social media. The beats (physical) and the words (mental) work together. That mind-body connection is what we're practicing in class, at game speed, so that we can activate it out in the real world. And once we connect our minds and bodies, we start to move our spirits and souls. The idea is that the music will help ensure that no matter what our frame of mind was when we came into class, it *will* be improved by the time we leave it.

This connection and the transformation start with the playlist. Because of the importance of the playlists, I work really hard at putting them together based on the kind of class I'll be instructing—raw hip-hop for the intense workouts, lighter tunes for the more chill classes.

When it comes to the playlist, though, there is a more important element than just the type of class I'll be teaching or the ups and downs of a particular ride. When I'm setting a playlist up, I tap deeply into what I'm feeling, and I really drill down on those emotions. Every single song I select for a playlist connects to me, to something I've been through, something I'm going through, or something I'm about to be going through. My playlist is totally authentic. It has to be in order for it to work.

But, like I said, the classes aren't real life. They are practice—or, in other words, preparation—for what we do in real life. And here's where the bigger reverberations come into play: the call to action. We need to be prepared for every day, to set our vibe so that we can be ready for anything and ready to achieve anything. In a bigger sense, it's about getting our minds right, creating the backbone for our day that will allow us to maximize any opportunities that come our way. It's about planning ahead and looking at what we have coming up and getting our minds right for it, how we set up the day around the "hills" we will face and making sure we have a "cooldown" period. One way to activate that is to *set your playlist.*

We can set our playlist in a lot of different ways. The goal is to work through a playlist that will improve our frame of mind, will clarify our thoughts and actions, and help align the mind and the body. And it has to be authentic to us. It might entail actually coming up with a musical playlist that you listen to throughout the day. It can be writing down things that become like little shots of espresso: a list of to-dos and goals for the day, motivational quotes or little affirmations or the things we are grateful for. It can be a morning workout. It can be literal meditation. The important thing is to have a plan and set the mood.

One way I set my own playlist outside of class: I create a "starting five" for each day.

I look at it through the prism of sports. I view each of the fifty-two weeks of a year as a "season," and each individual day as a "game" played against a different opponent. I am the coach of my team, and for every one of those "games," I set up a different starting lineup of priorities so that I have the best chance to win the day.

This starting lineup is composed of things or people, basically my priorities for that day. For instance, on one day, my starting five might be: (1) my overall mental and physical health, (2) my family, (3) my work and business, (4) my discipline and focus, and (5) my overall peace.

As the coach, it's my job to figure out the best starting five for each day. During any given week, priorities change, so I rotate and substitute. Maybe a friend or a girlfriend becomes a priority one day, so I'll analyze which "starters" I can sub them in for.

Throughout the week, I will make more adjustments to the starting lineup. The idea is to allow myself recovery time and to operate at maximum efficiency every day, and to do this all with intention and forethought—that preparation allows me to learn and grow and seize opportunity.

Another way to look at this is as if each day starts with one of those power strips that have five outlets on them. What I do is figure out which five things I can plug in that day—things that need power and energy and—importantly—things that will work together without tripping a circuit. I am generating my energy. But I am also protecting it.

Literally anything can make the starting lineup. Does one of my dogs need attention? Do I have a big meeting? Do I need to relax? Am I reading a book that requires more focus?

And literally all starters need some time on the bench, in order to get refreshed and recharged.

You know by now how much I love my mom. She is probably the most frequent starter on my daily team, my superstar player. But there are even times when I have to put her on the bench, just for a day or two, to prioritize something else that needs immediate attention or just to ensure that there is no burnout.

The best thing about all of this is that our playlist is something that we control. There is so much thrown at us every day in life that we cannot control, but the playlist is a way to take ownership of and agency over our own lives and not just passively let it happen to us.

By setting up a playlist, we exert some influence on the vibe for the day and the direction we want to take it. We need to identify our own starting five—is it our job, our marriage, our kids, our health? It's sort of like a systems check in our car. Look for what's working smoothly and also for what needs a tune-up or even an overhaul. Make a list of what motivates you and what's bringing you down. Put it all down on paper. If we set it up well, we'll be ready for any curveballs that come at us and ready when it comes time to riff and find that higher frequency.

• • •

When I was growing up, my mom always told me that I should seek out a wide variety of friends and hang out with people from different walks of life. Back then, I didn't really understand what she was getting at. But partly by design and partly by happenstance, that's pretty much what I ended up doing, especially as a kid.

In Coram, I hung out with the kids of recent immigrants, primarily from the Caribbean. In East Hampton, I was immersed in a town and a school system of fairly well-off white kids. At military school, I was exposed to all of those kids with their different backgrounds and dispositions.

And when I took on the extra classes at Flywheel and started traveling around New York City and instructing at different studios, I also came across all kinds of people. On the Upper East Side, the classes were mostly white moms. The Upper West Side had some grandmas. The Flatiron studio attracted the professional set—women and men in their twenties and thirties. The Chelsea studio had a mix of young white women, Black women, and gay men. (This mix of different people in different classes was fun for a lot of reasons. It kept the classes fresh, and it forced me to be creative with my playlists. Lots of Michael Jackson for the uptown classes; Kendrick Lamar and Biggie for the downtown ones, etc.)

When I started instructing all of these different demographics at Flywheel, I remembered my mom's advice to me as a kid and I started to understand *why* she had said it. When we hang out with and get to know a bunch of different types of people, we start to understand them—how they operate, where they've come from, and what motivates them. We start to see beyond the labels—the skin color, the political affiliations, the socioeconomics—and we start to realize that though we are all different, we are all of the same tribe, in a sense. When it's all boiled down and the nonsense and negativity are overcome, we all basically want the same things out of life—love and respect, for starters. We start to see that there is greatness in everyone and that, if and when that greatness is activated, we would all be better off, as individuals and as a society.

The thing, too, is that all of that exposure to different types of people can help us understand ourselves better. We all have our differences as well as our commonalities. Hanging around different people has helped me see that in myself. And it's helped me learn how to express myself and be authentic. Authentic expression is the way in which we define both our differences and our similarities, and how we make those things part of our strength.

• • •

Eventually, the bus rides back and forth to East Hampton started to become counterproductive—the hours in traffic, living out of a suitcase while shuffling between Jerome's floor and Grace's couch. Ruth suggested I give up the classes in East Hampton and move full-time to the city, where I could still easily teach twenty-five classes a week, but with a bit more sanity.

I was game.

I started looking around for a place to live. On Craigslist, I found a room in a duplex that seemed like it would work. The duplex was in Bushwick, Brooklyn, a traditionally working-class neighborhood that was just on the verge of becoming hip with the young professional set. I didn't know my roommates when I moved in—Craigslist didn't provide much information—and, truth be told, I found some of them to be a little strange when I did actually meet them. But, thankfully, I was working so much that I rarely saw my roommates. I had a place with a bed that wasn't too far away from work, and that was my main focus.

And, anyway, things were getting so crazy with my job that I didn't really even have time to think about them. It was all going well beyond what I had ever dreamed, really. The spin boom was continuing, reaching new heights. I was riding a bike for a living, playing the music I wanted to play, hitting it as hard as I could by getting myself into the right mindset every day. And people were starting to dig what I was doing. With every revolution I turned on the pedals, I was feeling good and starting to look good. My inner light was starting to shine through.

The classes started to have kind of a velvet rope atmosphere to them. They were selling out immediately after being posted online, and some people were even paying to be on the waitlist.

It was hard for me to truly grasp all of it. I sometimes had a hard time believing that I was actually teaching classes to begin with, much less that people were paying to come to them. A lot of the people who came to my classes were very successful, at the top of their respective games. And they were coming to be motivated by me, someone who, just a short while ago, was failing at everything he did, pretty much on the opposite end of the spectrum.

Flywheel continued to grow. A few months after I moved to New York City, Ruth started sending me around the country to help with this expansion. I went to Los Angeles to teach classes as a guest instructor. I traveled to Miami to open a new studio.

In the winter of 2012, Ruth asked me to do her a favor. Flywheel was set to open a studio in Dubai. She explained that the city was an important new outpost for the company and a great spot for a Flywheel studio—it was growing as an international destination, money was pouring in, and because of the hot and humid weather, people there were already used to working out indoors. She asked me if I would go over there for two weeks and train the instructors and help open up the studio. It was a big moment for me. No one had ever trusted me with something this big and important.

I went to Dubai and spent two hardworking weeks training the staff and then opening the studio. It was a blast.

• • •

That first year of instructing at Flywheel was a blur. I was feeling good and turning that into pure hustle, working as much as I could. I was making some money for the first time in my life, but more than that, I was becoming rich in purpose. That was my currency.

When I first started at Flywheel, I thought it would be just a job, that I would work, make money, and then go home. But it turned out to be so much more than that. I didn't realize what I would be getting back in return. When a rider told me that my class helped them be a better parent or a better person, I felt gratitude. My fear of failure receded. I started to shed my regret. My classes and the future I saw before me filled me with so much purpose. I was viewing myself as who I wanted to be, not what I used to be, and focusing on the present and a future. I settled on a few goals that gave my journey shape: I wanted to someday be able to retire my mom and give her the permanent break from work that she so deserved. And I wanted to prove to my dad that I wasn't a piece of shit.

In my second year at Flywheel, I could feel something *more* growing and building with each class. I was feeling different, moving different, waking up different, in a state of awe with what was going on around me. In my classes, I was using the pain and trauma I had been through to get motivated. That pain manifested itself as power. In every single class, I projected that energy, and in every single class, the riders were using my verve to help them create their own power.

I had started to look good to myself. It has zero to do with what I looked like on the outside. I had an internal vibe, an inner light. And **once we glow internally, we start to shine externally.** It is impossible to ignore.

And there was a rebound effect. Our internal lights shine

externally and help power the lights of other people. In turn, those lights come back to help power ours. I felt good and looked good. I motivated people, which made them motivated and feel good. And that vibe came right back at me. Remember the energetic grocery bagger. When we shine internally and externally, we start to get it all back, in spades.

CHAPTER 8

MAKE YOUR FREE THROWS

One of the things we do when we are merely existing and not living is to miss, outright, the things that are right in front of us. These are the things that are accessible to us, but we are unable to receive them, for whatever reason. Maybe we're caught up in worry or negativity. Maybe we don't feel good or look good and thus are unable to practice gratitude and unable to be receptive to anything outside of our own heads. I call these things that are right in front of us "free throws." And in life, it's vitally important to *make your free throws*.

Yes, another basketball analogy. Let me explain.

I'll start with the literal meaning, as in shots taken in a basketball game from a line fifteen feet from the basket by a player who has been fouled by someone on the opposing team. In the game of basketball, dunks and three-point shots get all of the glory on the highlight reels, but many games are literally won or lost on free throws. So many basketball games come down to the last few minutes, and almost all of those games are decided by which team makes more of the free throws down the stretch.

Take the four-time NBA champion Steph Curry. Picture him standing at the free throw line. He is in his opponent's arena. There are two seconds left in the game. His team is down by one point. He has two free throw attempts. The outcome of the game literally rests in his hands.

He is sweating and exhausted from the effort he has put into the game up to this point. The fans of the home team are screaming as loudly as they can and are waving their arms and jumping up and down in his line of sight behind the backboard, trying to do anything they can to distract him.

When it comes to the raw score of the game, those last free throws that Steph is about to take are no more important than the ones he took when he was fouled in the game's first two minutes. But in the broader scheme of things, his free throws at that moment mean so much more than any other shots he's taken during the game and anything else he's done during the game. The outcome hangs in the balance. Circumstances matter.

Steph, like all the greats, is ready for this moment. His discipline helps him override and ignore the distraction of the fans, and helps him slow down and go through his routine so that he will be able to make the best stroke he can on his shots. He has stayed in the gym after practice and worked on his free throws, with the actual game in mind, shooting practice free throws with music blaring and teammates all waving their hands. He has gone through the same routine on every free throw he takes: Stare at the basket, envision the ball going in. Take a deep breath. Dribble the ball once. Step up to the line. Take another dribble. And then shoot. Steph famously never leaves a practice session until he makes five swishes—that is, the ball touching nothing but net—on ten made free throws. That, he says, "sets the bar for how you want to see the ball go through the basket every time."

That's what practicing at game speed is all about.

Steph is known and celebrated for his spectacular three-point shots. He is the best ever at making them. But a lesser-known fact about Steph is that, because of the work and attention he has put in, he has become the best free throw shooter of all time. His three-pointers made him famous. His ability to hit free throws, though an unheralded aspect of his game, made him great.

All of that practice he puts in on his free throws provides him with the chance to take advantage of the opportunity that has been presented to him. He won't make them all. That's impossible. But he's put himself in the position to make most of them.

Our free throws in life come in different forms. They can be the things that have been given to us, things over which we have some agency—our family, our health, our privilege. They can be things that have been given to us over which we have little or no agency—the kindness of strangers, luck. Our duty, like Steph in the practice gym, is to be ready to receive them when they are presented to us. The idea is that they are unimpeded—the defense isn't in our face. It's up to us to make them.

I was not making my free throws for a large part of my life. I had the privilege of a family that made sacrifices for me. I had the privilege of great friends, like Jerome, who gave me love and asked for nothing in return. I wasn't prepared to make those free throws. I wasn't ready to receive the success they signaled.

I finally got ready when I started to feel good about myself. By learning to love and trust myself, I learned how to love and trust others and, by doing so, could make the free throws that were presented to me. I "practiced" for them by taking the small steps, by being present with myself and finding gratitude. And as I practiced more and more, I got better at making my free throws.

Jayvee's offer to me to come work as a janitor at Flywheel was a free throw. Jerome's family was a free throw. Ruth having the faith in me to try out as an instructor was a free throw. The positive feedback I got on the bike was a free throw.

Take a minute here to think about the free throws we all might have in our lives. One of our children asking us to read them a story. The ability we have to call our parents and check in on them whenever we want. The opportunity we have to smile and say a warm hello to our coworkers when we reach the office. That five minutes we will be giving ourselves every morning to get it started right. Little things that all have big meaning.

I was lucky enough to have been given the time and the grace to figure out that I had been given free throws, that things had been presented to me. That realization made me better equipped to stand on that line and make them. It's made me better at making them ever since.

We don't have to make spectacular dunks or three-pointers from a crazy-long range to be great in life. We just have to pay attention to the little things—receive them, embrace them, and make the most of them.

Finally, being able to make my free throws led to a job that would change my life.

• • •

Midway through 2015, I was two years into my instructing job at Flywheel. I was digging it. I was learning something in every class. I loved helping motivate people, and I fed off of the response I received. I loved my coworkers. And I loved my boss.

One day, that boss called me into her office.

"Alex, I wanted to give you the heads-up on something. Something important," Ruth said.

She told me that I should expect a call soon from a company called Peloton. She had talked to the people there, and they were going to try to hire me.

I was in shock and was a little bit confused. *Was Ruth unhappy with my work? Was she trying to get rid of me?*

No, she told me. She was looking out for me.

I shook my head. "No, Ruth, I'm rocking with you. I'm loyal to you and I have no desire to go anywhere else." I didn't even know what Peloton was. Never heard of it.

Ruth explained that Peloton was a start-up with some serious funding. She knew some of the people behind it and thought they were very good at what they did.

"Alex, I wanted to tell you about this because I think it's something you should strongly consider," she said. "And I don't want to ever hold you back from opportunities and growth. This one could be a life changer."

After I left her office, I was still in a bit of a daze. Most bosses, it seemed to me, would have recoiled at the thought of losing an employee to another company, especially one in the same space. But Ruth wasn't like that, and that's what made her who she was. Mom first, boss second. She knew that I had plans to one day take care of *my* mom. She knew that I felt like I still had something to prove to my dad. And she knew that this might just be my opportunity to do both of those things.

The call I received from Peloton turned out to be from a familiar person. It was Jayvee . . . the same Jayvee who had helped keep me alive when I was a kid and then hired me for the janitor job at Flywheel. She had become my guardian angel and, in a way, helped me start understanding what doing better—looking out for and helping others—really meant.

On the phone, Jayvee explained what had set all of this in motion. Looking for a new challenge, she had left Flywheel in 2013 and had joined Peloton a year later. The start-up company not only had big money, but it also had big aspirations.

She told me that the chief content officer at Peloton at the time, a man named Fred Klein, had asked his staff to research the spin scene. A few weeks later, Jayvee told me, Fred had a follow-up meeting with his staff to get feedback on what everyone had discovered. He went around the room as people presented their thoughts. At one point, Fred asked, "Anyone know this Alex guy at Flywheel?" Jayvee, who is now the vice president of community at Peloton, said she sat there in silence, wanting to speak up, but not sure if she should, because of our friendship. But before she could make up her mind about what to do, a colleague turned to her and said, "He went to East Hampton High School. Did you know him?"

She said yes, and Fred asked her to get in touch with me.

A few days after our call, Jayvee and I met in a little bar in the East Village. It was great to catch up with her—I hadn't seen her in a while, and she had played an integral role in my life. We eventually got around to Peloton. She laid it all out for me: It was a spin company and would have classes, just like SoulCycle and Flywheel, but most riders would be on their bikes in their homes, doing the classes via livestream. Peloton, she explained, was much smaller than Flywheel (at the time), but its potential was enormous. If things went according to plan, classes could generate tens of thousands—if not someday hundreds of thousands—of riders.

I was initially a little skeptical of instructing without being in the same room as the vast majority of the riders. (Peloton planned to have a small number of riders in the studio, a plan they would eventually execute.) The energy of a live class is just so pure. But I was intrigued enough to entertain the idea.

Jayvee went back to Fred and told him I was interested. Fred then took me to lunch in the city. He filled me in on Peloton's grand plans and then gave me the hard sell. He flattered me. He told me that with my voice, I could do voice-overs for a living. He told me that Ruth had sung my praises. And then he challenged me: Why would I settle for instructing classes of fifty people when I could instruct classes a hundred times that size?

After that lunch, he put me in touch with John Foley, the

founder and, at the time, CEO of Peloton. I met John first at the company headquarters on Park Avenue, and then later at his home in the Hamptons. John was straight with me: Though the company had huge potential and he was incredibly confident that it would fulfill that potential, nothing was a given in the start-up world. He then offered me a job.

I had a decision to make, the biggest one of my life up until then. I had failed at everything in my life, and then, in the nick of time, had found something I was good at and loved doing. That thought—I had been on the precipice of being a total failure but had somehow hung on, not fallen, and had even started to climb up—made my heart race. My decision boiled down to this: I could rest on my laurels and keep doing what I was doing. Or I could take a risk and push myself to grow and progress.

As I ruminated about it all, I thought about the courage it took for my parents to come to the United States in search of a better life without even being able to speak the language. I thought about how much they had sacrificed over the years, about how I had come so close to squandering everything they'd done for me. I thought about how privileged I was in that sense. Crazy privileged. I had found a path to work hard. But was I going hard enough? (I still wonder that to this day.) All of those thoughts made my heart race, too.

I thought about what it would take to make a leap of faith, to truly put myself to the test. The Peloton job had its obvious risks, and it would be sort of like starting over in my career, though certainly not from the bottom. I talked to my parents and Ruth. I talked to other friends. I actually turned down the job a few times—I just wasn't sure about it. I was in a comfort zone. I wasn't scared of growing, but I had done so much and overcome so much to get out of such a negative space and find my groove. I was a bit worried that a new job, especially one with some risks, might put me in danger of falling back.

One night I sat in the basement of my Brooklyn apartment, watching the Miami Heat in the NBA playoffs. I had talked to Ruth earlier that day and had told her that I didn't think I was going to take the job at Peloton.

And then I saw an ad for Peloton featuring Robin Arzón, the current vice president of fitness instruction and the head instructor for the company. She seemed to be looking me dead in the eye. *Oh shit*, I thought. It felt like a sign, like God or fate was telling me something, and telling me loud and clear. We can't block our own blessings.

I took the job the next day.

I didn't know it at the time, but there was one potential roadblock that stood in my way. There was a big investor at Flywheel—he had some pull because of the size of the investment—who didn't want me to leave for a rival spin company. He wanted to protect his assets. He demanded that Ruth block the deal. But Ruth, in yet another act of graciousness toward me, stood up to the investor and told him that I was free to do whatever I wanted. The guy eventually backed down.

It was November 2015. I had one last conversation with Ruth before I officially signed the Peloton papers. She simply told me: "I think we both know you have to give this a shot." Ruth was as good as they come, the epitome of what it means to be a great boss. She actually cared about her employees and thought not only about what they could do for her, but also about what they could do for themselves.

And with that, I officially left Flywheel and became an instructor at Peloton.

• • •

"Fake it 'til you make it" is something you hear people say all the time. This is bad advice. In fact, I would suggest the opposite: *Don't fake it 'til you make it*. Because faking it—at any time—is the wrong mindset.

The best athletes, singers, CEOs, grocery baggers, and janitors do not fake it. They're authentic, and that authenticity makes them the best they can be.

When John hired me, he gave me one mandate, one that was strikingly similar to what Ruth had told me when I started instructing at Flywheel: "Be yourself, Alex. Let it fly."

This, of course, made me very happy. It is such a great thing to hear from a boss or a family member or a friend. The reason it's so great? It perfectly aligns with what we should be doing anyway. The toughest job in the world is being fake, because we have to wake up every day and remember that lie, or adjustment, that we've been telling ourselves. Just be you. Don't pretend, don't be a phony, don't imitate, don't brag, don't falsify. Don't *try* to be an original. Just be yourself and you will be. A lot of people will accept us for who we are. Some won't, and that's OK. It's mainly their problem. Be real, be true to ourselves. We sleep better that way, I promise.

As nice as that was to hear from John, though, I didn't need it. We don't need someone else to tell us to be ourselves, to give us that green light. We are the ones who decide that and decide to express it to the world.

Being authentic was the only way I knew how to be when it came to the bike. I took the military school discipline, the cadence of all of the marching and drilling I'd done, my voice, my experiences, my love of music, and the ability to connect and communicate with a broad range of people, and folded them all into one package. We are all the sum of our experiences. On the bike, I express who I am. I don't try to be anyone else. I play the music that I listen to, the songs that move me. Yes, some of them are risqué, but that is real and authentic, too, to me and to the stories the music tells. I put my purpose and intent and heart and soul into it all.

I do this now when I'm not on the bike, too. The bike has prepared me to do it in real life, as well.

Authenticity is our source of power, our source of being.

The thing is, we can't pretend to be someone or something we're not and also truly activate our greatness.

I was faking it through my entire life until I got that first job at Flywheel. I faked my way through school. I faked looking good—it was only on the outside. I faked my smile. I faked my way through my relationship with my dad. I faked that I was OK.

With that janitor job, I stopped. I brought myself to that job every single day. That was *me* mopping those floors. That was *me* who got the instructor job and led those classes. That was *me* who got hired by Peloton. The bottom line is this: I didn't "make it" until I stopped faking it.

A lot of people use the phrase "fake it 'til you make it" when, say, they are getting a new job or trying something new. The idea is to pretend or try to pull one over on someone else—like a boss—until we figure it all out. Again, I just don't think this is the right thing to do. The idea should be, instead, to bring ourselves to the job or the task, and not even think about faking it. "All you can do is show up as your most authentic self," as Mel Robbins, author of *The 5 Second Rule*, says.

CHAPTER 9

DO NOT OUTSOURCE YOUR GREATNESS

True greatness is not activated by others. It's done by ourselves.

The path to activating our greatness has plenty of roadblocks. Trust me. I've had head-on collisions with all of them. Many of those roadblocks don't necessarily have to do with us per se, but instead have to do with the relationship between our inner, true self and other people. All of us allow other people to define us, in real life and on social media. We look to them to tell us we're great, whether that's in person or through "likes" and heart emojis.

We don't need others to tell us we're great, to validate us. We need to do it ourselves. *Do not outsource your greatness*. I let myself be defined by others for a good portion of my life. I doubted my own self-worth and greatness. And there is no heavier resistance in life than doubt.

I want to tell you how I stopped doing that and, in the process, took a giant step in activating my own greatness.

. . .

Leaving Flywheel to join Peloton came with a stipulation: I had a noncompete that stemmed from my prior contract, which meant I would have to wait three months before starting at Peloton. My new company told me that I should consider those three months a vacation and take the time off to heal my body—which I had put under some duress for three straight years—and to clear my mind. I started getting paid at signing, so I had the freedom to just chill.

But it turned out that I didn't want to. Almost immediately, I started to get restless. I missed the grind. I missed instructing classes and missed the interaction with the community. Being benched, albeit for a good reason, sucks. Period.

Being in the city and not teaching only amplified that restlessness. So I decided to leave New York for a bit. I flew out to Los Angeles to link up with a friend, Archie Archibong, someone I'd met in the city. He'd graduated from engineering school at Columbia University and was working at a tech start-up.

But even out there, with the welcome change of scenery, I remained antsy. Peloton expected me to take those three months off and chill and then enter their training program. But I decided that I'd do something different.

Instead, I started to train myself in the Peloton method. My idea was to be ready for work on day one. Behind the scenes, I signed up for Peloton and started taking classes. I studied the instructors, analyzing the overall shape of the classes and making note of how and when they looked into the camera to connect and interact with the riders. I calculated the intervals and the climbs, and paid close attention to the cadences used during those climbs and on the flat parts of the ride. I studied these rides with the focus and intensity that I should have had while in school or basketball practice.

In the back of my mind, I felt like I had some responsibility to not just work hard at this, but also to outwork it. I didn't exactly feel pressure to do it but felt something more like a duty. At age twenty-three, I was the youngest instructor that Peloton had signed, and I wanted to prove to the company that they had made the right decision by recruiting me and that I belonged with the top instructors in the world. But the bigger reason I outworked it was that I was Peloton's first and only Black instructor. I felt like the impression I made at Peloton—within the company and with the riders—was somehow about much more than just me. This was something—this duty to represent something more than just myself—that I would think about in a much deeper way later on in my Peloton career.

At the end of those three months, I flew back east and reported to Peloton's headquarters. I met with the training instructor, Christine D'Ercole. She asked me what I knew, if anything, about the Peloton instructing method.

"I don't need training," I told her. "I'm ready to contribute right away."

She was dubious, I could tell.

As proof, I asked for a test. I asked her to throw together a random playlist of songs, and then I would show her what I could do. So she did. I hopped on the bike. She played three random songs and I "taught" a class.

When I was done, she left the room, saying she was going to

"talk to someone." When she came back, she informed me that I could skip the training.

I was struck by how . . . nice she was about it. It dawned on me then that while the preparation I did for this "test" was spot on, the way I approached that actual day was a bit off. I had the wrong mindset. I came in all hotheaded, trying to prove something to her and to Peloton, like some sort of rogue. I felt competitive. What I didn't realize is that Christine—and Peloton—were there to actually *help* me. We were a team, and I was *already* part of it. We worked together and lifted each other up.

It was the first lesson I learned on the job at Peloton, and it's one I've never forgotten.

. . .

My initial Peloton class was February 3, 2016. My mindset for that class was simple: *I want to hit these people with something they've never seen before.* The red light of the camera went on. I was live. Jay-Z started rapping through the speakers. . . .

I remember the feeling I had when the red light flicked off and I stepped off the bike that day. I *had* succeeded in bringing something different, as Ruth said I would. Every instructor at Peloton was great—John and Fred and Jayvee and the rest had, in fact, done an incredible job of recruiting the best spin instructors in the land. But I brought something else to the table. Not better. Just different and authentic to me. No one had my background. No one brought what I did to class. "Nobody built like you / you designed yourself," as Jay-Z said in "A Dream," which was the first song I ever played at Peloton.

I ran with that feeling.

I still had a lot to learn, though. The Peloton experience was different from the Flywheel one, for sure. While there were some riders in the studio when I joined, the platform was built on live-streaming and on-demand "coach-to-camera" content. That took some getting used to. You don't get that huge, instant reflected vibe that you do when you have a full studio. It's kind of the same experience you have when doing a Zoom or other type of virtual "calls" as opposed to in-person meetings (except that, in my case, I couldn't see the people on the other side of the camera).

I had to learn how to utilize my motivation in a different way, to get myself ready and in the right frame of mind to work hard and find intensity while I was essentially by myself, to find the motivation and then sustain it on my own. I did that by looking into the camera and visualizing someone out there, riding a bike in her attic, looking for help and the motivation to maximize her opportunities in this thirty-minute session. I had my monitor, and while I couldn't see faces, I could see—through avatars and numbers—who was out there working hard, coming back to class after class, hitting personal records.

I came to learn that the camera, in a peculiar but very real way, could create *more* intimacy than a live class. It made me appear as if I was closer to the individual rider, and speaking to him or her individually. There was a lot of power in that.

The storytelling, I learned, was different, too. Your emotions are much easier to read in real life, in front of people—you can make big, exaggerated gestures with your arms, for instance, to get something across to those in the room. But on video, with that more intimate feel of a close-up camera, you have to emote mainly with your face, with expressions, and with variations in your voice. It's kind of the difference between stage and movie acting. What that means, in the end, is that you have to embody your emotions more, really absorb them, and then project them outward.

All of that, as it turned out, suited me very well. Instructing at Peloton to a camera forced me—really, freed me up—to go deeper into what I was feeling. That helped me, too, on a personal level, with my self-examination, which improved my overall mental health. In the process, it would provide me with the chance to help others do the same.

That said, for my first few months at Peloton, I went as hard as I could and was still a bit of a hothead. My classes were physical, athletic, and tough. In feeding off my raw emotions, I was teaching for the body. I hadn't quite figured out yet how to teach for the mind. I think a lot of people make this same mistake, particularly early on in their careers.

I treated every class as an audition (and still do), for myself, for the riders, and for someone else who wasn't in class that day. I wanted everyone to have such a transformative experience that they would go tell their friends about it. That way, I thought, I wouldn't just add riders. I would multiply them.

Though this was great, it was also exhausting—I felt like I was sprinting all the time. We all did. Peloton was growing at hyperspeed, well on its way to becoming the largest interactive fitness brand in the world. Literally everything John and Fred and Jayvee had told me would happen, did happen. In fact, it was

happening faster than they said it would. They had underprom-
ised and overdelivered.

I didn't realize at the time that, in some senses, it was all going
a bit too fast, that I had been neglecting some things within me
that needed to be addressed. All of that changed rather abruptly
with one phone call.

· · ·

To this point, the arc of my relationship with my dad went from
being great pals when I was really young, with him even spoiling
me at times, to him getting sick and everything starting to go awry.
I never lost respect for him, but when I was sent off to military
school and for the years following that, we disconnected almost
completely, only dealing with each other with rage and hatred,
which culminated on that Thanksgiving Day, when he told me
what he really thought of me.

But after I got the job at Flywheel, there was a slight shift. He
never really inquired about anything or asked how I was doing
or anything like that. But the fire of his fury toward me seemed
to have waned. He just seemed sort of disinterested. Maybe the
fact that I had steady work and he saw me hustling took a little of
the sting out of his anger toward me. I would never know how he
really felt, though. He never expressed himself that way. He was
still that clenched fist.

During my "no days off" period at Flywheel, I was in East
Hampton on the weekends. I would sometimes stop by the house
to say a brief hello, usually when I knew my mom was there. I

would even, on rare occasions, spend the night there if I needed a place to crash. My dad and I found a way to coexist somewhat peaceably during those short visits. There was always tension—when I had dinner with my mom and him, there was always something bubbling up just under the surface that felt like it could erupt with very little prompting. But, by then, I could keep it together, at least long enough to get out of the house without an incident. I purposely kept any interactions with him as short as they could be.

My pain—which has become my inspiration—has a lot of sources. My failures, my problems at school, etc. But by the time I was instructing at Flywheel, it came mainly from my dad. Some of that pain started when he was sick and when, even as a six-year-old, I realized that he might disappear from this earth for good at any moment. But most of it came from the anguish of our relationship after he got sick, all of the hatred that spewed from both of us.

By the time I got to Peloton, though, I had been out of the house for years. I was living in Brooklyn and didn't interact with him much, if at all, seeing him maybe once every few months. I felt too good by then to allow him to mess with my vibe. I believed that I had effectively removed him from my vision, that he was no longer the focal point of my pain, of my life. I told myself that I kept him only in the back of my mind.

But I was lying to myself.

He was still there, still front and center. I still did everything I did with him in mind, consciously or subconsciously. And, in that way, he was still the most important person in my life. All of which made what happened next even more impactful, but not necessarily in the way I had always envisioned it would be.

• • •

On April 4, 2016, almost exactly two months after I had started at Peloton, I taught two classes, one at 9:30 A.M. and the other at 6:30 P.M. After that last class, I walked outside of Peloton's Chelsea studio into a sixty-five-degree early spring evening. I was wearing a hoodie and shorts and had my backpack on. I was feeling good. Physically, I was pleasantly tired, my muscles loose and relaxed. Mentally, I was on the high that usually lasts an hour or two after every class.

I was headed to the subway, back out to Brooklyn, when my phone rang. I saw my dad's name pop up, which was unusual. He rarely called me. I kept walking as I answered it. He said hello and immediately started talking, just some small talk about who he had seen in the neighborhood recently. *Weird*, I thought. *It's not like him just to call and chitchat.*

He paused for what seemed like an unnaturally long time. And then he started talking again. He told me that he had seen an article in his local paper about me and my work at Peloton. He paused again.

"Lex, I just want to let you know that I'm proud of you," he said. "You're doing it."

I immediately stopped in my tracks. I felt like I was having an out-of-body experience. I could hear the cars go by on the streets and the conversations of other people around me with an odd clarity. I snapped back to reality, squeaked out a quick "thanks," and then we said goodbye. I started to cry. Tears of joy, relief. I walked down the stairs to the subway in a complete daze and rode home, sitting on the seat. I listened to some music, but I have no recollection of which songs. When I got home, I threw my backpack on a chair, and it all hit me with a *boom*.

He validated me.

That thought left me elated for a moment. But then I started to feel a little confused, an emotion I couldn't figure out right away. A moment later, though, I realized why I felt that way: *I had never needed that validation to begin with.*

Though I felt good and was starting to look good by then, I realized at that moment that I had still been merely existing and not really living. I was just getting by. I was suppressing the positive things in my life, which is nearly as bad as suppressing the negative ones. And I realized how bad this had been for my mental health. Living my life this way—doing everything just to prove my dad wrong—was bad for me. It didn't allow me to grow, to fully live up to my potential, to be great.

I had been yearning for years for that very moment, that congratulations, that expression of pride. Once I got it, though, I wondered why I had been yearning for so long.

It came down to the doubt I felt about myself. I didn't feel worthy of being his son. This realization did a few things for me. First, it opened up an entire new level of empathy and sympathy for my dad. I started to fully realize his pain—caused by circumstance, by himself, and by me. But it had always been more about how he viewed *himself* and not much about how he viewed me. Realizing that helped me process all of those years of anguish.

I understood that despite the hatred and resentment I had felt toward him, I loved him and always had and always would. Both Jerome and Jared, when they were young, had lost their fathers to cancer. Both of them had reminded me many times over the years that you only get one dad, and that I should reconcile with mine sooner rather than later. I didn't understand what they were saying until that moment. I understood now that I loved my dad *because he was my dad*. Period.

But I also understood that I loved him because of what he had instilled in me. No, it wasn't pleasant. But a lot of the discipline, respect, and hard work within me had come from him, in one way or another. That protective shell I have—constructed, in many ways, because of him—not only allowed me to shield myself from pain and negativity, but it also allowed me to let the good things in, like love and light, all while protecting those things in the process.

I'm different because of my dad. I think differently and move differently. My belief in myself, which took decades to emerge, came, in an indirect way, from him, because of my burning desire to prove his assessment of me wrong. That assessment opened up my eyes about how I had played a significant role in the failures of my early life. It forced me to realize that I had to accept the consequences of my own actions and change those actions to become a better person and to treat others as I wanted to be treated. In the end, it all made me a better person. I learned how to transform pain into power.

I had finally realized that because I didn't have to prove him wrong anymore, I didn't have to doubt my own self-worth. That restriction had been lifted. I could really start to *live*.

And that made me realize that I didn't want to do all of this for myself. That wasn't my only purpose. My greater purpose was to do it for others.

For so long in my life, as a kid and even into manhood, I was desperately looking for someone to notice me, to validate me, to grab me and shake me and tell me I was great. I was looking for that from my teachers, from my drill sergeants. But, mostly, I was looking for it from my dad.

But I shouldn't have been waiting for him or for anyone else to do this.

I felt like all of my life I had been on a stage in a darkened theater. I thought I had been up there just rehearsing, and things didn't feel like they were going very well. I felt alone and lost.

And then one person—my dad—walked into the theater one day and told me he was proud of me . . . and, *wham*, the theater lights went on. And I looked into the seats and saw Ruth and Jerome and Jayvee and Coach Hartwell and my mom all in the front row. I looked back into the rest of the seats and realized that they all had people sitting in them. The theater had been full the entire time but I hadn't realized it. I couldn't see it through the darkness in my own head. And I wondered: *Why did I wait so long to do so?*

Outsourcing our greatness happens all of the time in our lives. We all look for this validation—from family, friends, coworkers, and even strangers. It's particularly hard to avoid doing it these days with a relatively new and easy and instantly gratifying way of seeking it out: in the virtual world.

Social media is here to stay. There is no putting that genie back into the bottle. I'm on it. It's likely you are, too. There are, without a doubt, some real positives to social media. It enables us to connect with our friends, make new friends, celebrate, commiserate, and even mourn. It can create a community, and that's a good thing.

But we should never ignore the negatives of social media, and there are some massive ones. We need to acknowledge those negatives and deal with them.

The biggest negative, I think, is that social media can quickly become a false reality. We've all heard this. We all know this. But I think we forget sometimes *why* this is a negative and how it can impact our lives.

When we post on social media, we want to be heard. That's the primal urge that makes these apps so powerful. We pay close attention to "likes" and "reposts" and all of those things that signal approval to us. And, a lot of times—we all do this—we look to those signals for validation of our own worth, our own greatness.

One of the biggest problems is that social media is merely a highlight show. Most of us only post the good stuff and not the real stuff—the failures, the grind. The algorithms favor the highlight approach. That's the false reality. I've seen this a lot in the fitness world, seen people preach motivation on social media and then put the phone down and retreat to the back room and break down and cry. That false reality is unhealthy.

We're human, but social media doesn't deal with real humanity very well. Social media does not favor the humble. That pressure to be perfect on social media is so distorting that when something bad does happen in real life, it makes it all worse. I want to be human. I don't want to be the guy who is always right. That's far too much pressure. I fuck up all the time. And when I do, I admit it and call myself out

My rule on social media is this: I always try to remember that it's a tool and that we should treat it as such. Of course, tools can be used for good and bad. But just remember that it's a tool. We must use it wisely.

Our greatness, on the other hand, is not just a tool we log in and out of. It's imperative we activate it, whether or not anyone is there to see it or like it or share it. And it can't be outsourced—to social media or anything or anyone else. It can only be sourced by us and us alone.

· · ·

April 4, 2016, taught me a few other things, as well. I learned that we should *hold ourselves above the BS . . . but not too far*. I held on to the negativity of my relationship with my dad too tightly and for too long. There is no benefit when something like that— something negative—consumes us or dominates our thoughts. However, there can be a benefit to remembering the BS, but in a practical, thoughtful way. You can keep it in a small pocket somewhere in your head for motivation, as a way of turning your pain into power. The trick here is to never let it out of that pocket, never get back under it. In other words, don't let it get in the way of your greatness.

We also have to *disconnect from negative energy sources*. We all have toxic relationships in some form or manner—at home, at work, in our lives. I bet you can think of one right now. It seems crazy and irrational, but we often hang on to these relationships. Maybe we hang on because of the natural urge to want to fix something that's broken, which is a noble thought but rarely works out. Or maybe we hang on to a bad relationship for nostalgia's sake or because of the time invested or because it's just become a bad habit that we can't quite shake. Maybe it's with a family member, or it's someone we've known for years and the inertia of the relationship keeps it going. There are also relationships that we kind of become addicted to because of the drama, the highs and lows.

Whatever the reason, if we come to realize that a relationship is a negative one, we need to unplug it. Immediately. Of course, it's never black and white. But if you keep it real with yourself about the overall plus/minus rating of the relationship, every day we wait to pull the plug increases the difficulty of unplugging it later and increases the damage done. Negative relationships are heavy anchors on our lives. They stanch our growth and evolution. They deplete our energy. And our energy is our most valuable resource.

Disconnecting from negative relationships is complicated and hard. I admit that I still have trouble with it. But one way I look at it is this: We have an alarm to protect our house and our car. We have a password to protect access to our phone. We need to also set up a security system for ourselves, especially when someone who is negative demands access. *Guard your heart, protect your mind* is a game-saving concept. There are some practical ways to do it: Mute or block the person on social media and your phone. Avoid the person in social situations. But what happens in your mind is more important. Condition yourself to deal with negative people and negative things by taking the time to think them through. Deal with the issue, figure out what the best course of action is, and then let it go. Don't get consumed with it. ***Don't ever let anyone steal your energy.***

When we disconnect from these negative relationships—free that anchor—we start to evolve and grow again. Disconnecting can be painful, of course, but it's vital. We are held back when we don't disconnect. We can't turn our pain into power if we're still fully plugged into the pain.

And it's important to keep some perspective. Disconnecting isn't always permanent. It can be in certain situations, and when it is, it becomes much clearer that we needed to disconnect in the first place. But a lot of times we disconnect, and then we evolve and grow without the relationship weighing us down. And the other person evolves and grows, too. And that, a lot of the time, makes it possible to reconnect, on better and healthier terms. This is exactly what I would eventually do with my dad.

. . .

After my dad's call, my classes at Peloton were just different. My Flywheel stage had been about me healing myself, getting over the negativity and the feelings of doubt to feel good. Peloton had been about the process of looking good. I had healed and started to really like what I was seeing in myself. And, after I was released from the motivation of trying to prove my dad wrong—and once I realized that it was never the point to begin with—something else was released.

One of the most important concepts in my bike instruction is the concept of *validation*. A spin class puts us in motion, starting with the warmup. And then we tackle big hills, hit the intervals. We work and outwork in every class. In every class, I see people pushing themselves and hitting personal records. And I think it is hugely important—and motivating—to recognize these achievements, and to do so in real time. To validate them.

Validation is about seeing progress as it happens and marking those moments. During class, after working through, say, a big hill, I ask the riders: "How do you view yourself in this moment right now? Think about how you viewed yourself in minute zero as opposed to now, minute twelve, after that climb. Two different people, right?"

The roar in the warmup (virtually or nonvirtually) is always pretty solid. We are ready to get to work. But the roar after we've climbed the hill, and made all of that progress and validated it, is always immensely louder. The gap between how we viewed ourselves in the beginning and how we view ourselves after we validated the climb is the result of the work we've done and the fact that we acknowledged it. We feel good, and because of that, we look good. We can *see* the results. Acknowledging—or validating—that greatness is such a key. It makes it so much more powerful. And it creates a habit—muscle and mental memories—that we can reach back to and access when we need it, when we don't feel like our best selves.

I talked earlier about how important it is for us to acknowledge our negativity and negative emotions, to confront and deal with the things that are bringing us down and holding us back.

Not doing so—suppressing them—only means they will come back stronger and haunt us.

It's equally important not to suppress the positive things and moments in our lives, as well. We all do this all of the time, and it can be as bad for us as suppressing the negative. We need to celebrate the good things that happen to us and not just let them pass by, unrecognized. When we suppress the positive, we enter the danger zone—we shrink ourselves back into places we've outgrown. We fall back into holes filled with bad habits and negativity.

Instead, we need to validate the positive, in real time. Validation helps us get more out of the positivity. When we ask ourselves: "Are we doing it?" and the answer is "Yes," validate it then and there. Because progress can be so painfully slow, validating it becomes all the more important. Had a great day? Validate it. Good night's sleep? Validate it. Did your kid give you a great hug? Validate it. Did you lose two pounds in one week? Validate it.

The more we validate the good things, the better we get at doing so and the more we turn validating into a habit that can help us overcome negativity.

Now, let's be clear: This does not mean going around and telling everyone how great we are. It's not about beating our chests in public. That's not validation. That's shallow bragging. We don't even need to say it out loud to anyone. We just need to feel it and recognize it.

Feeling good is our warmup and our climb. Looking good is validating what we've accomplished. And once we've reached that place, we're ready for the next giant step. We're ready to look out onto the larger world, to help amplify the positive and help overcome the negative. We've helped ourselves. Now we're ready to help others.

• • •

Within a few months after that phone call from my dad, my entire vibe, on and off the bike, evolved even more. I began to share more of myself and my story. I began to teach more for the mind and spirit and soul than I did for the body. I looked good and felt good internally—my frequency was at an all-time high. Which was good because now, with every class and with all of my days, I came to realize that what I truly wanted was for everyone who came into contact with me to feel what I was feeling.

I desired that because I had been in those dark places, where it seems like no one understands you or understands what you're thinking. That was the reason I went so hard. It's the reason I go so hard to this day, that I'm so passionate about my purpose. I refuse to allow anyone to come to my class—or this book, for that matter—feeling the way I used to feel, and then leave feeling the same way.

There would be other significant and different mountaintops I would climb in the future, but I had reached my first summit. And I was ready for the next step on my journey.

I was ready to do better.

CHAPTER 10

VIBE CHECK

I want to pause here for just a moment to talk a bit about some characteristics that I think we can all work on that will help us ascend that mountain and feel good, look good, and eventually do better.

There are, of course, a ton of character traits that we should strive to have and embody. Some are pretty obvious: Be kind. Be grateful. Treat others like you want to be treated. Don't obsess about what others think of you. Etcetera, etcetera. But I want to home in on three characteristics that I think are absolutely critical to our journey.

The first is *curiosity*.

Curiosity is a mindset. It's a way in which we advance our knowledge about ourselves and the world. It's a key component in our personal growth. Being curious allows us to add another layer and evolve. It plays a huge role in our everyday lives—in our work and in our family lives and relationships.

Being curious requires effort. It means pushing ourselves, testing our limits. Our natural inclination is to live and operate within our own comfort zones. But doing this means we are existing and not living. It makes us stale and stalls our growth.

Curiosity takes us out of that comfort zone, and it opens up an entirely new level of living and not just existing. It opens up all kinds of new doors of opportunity. It helps us along the journey of feeling good and looking good. And it also helps us when we reach the destination of doing better.

Being curious doesn't mean just chasing the next thing blindly, careening wildly from one thing to the next. It's done with thought and purpose and intention.

A few years after I started at Peloton, I created the Do Better Foundation with my business partners, Dave Park and Archie Archibong. I have huge ambitions for the foundation, but I knew we had to get the ball rolling with something manageable and tangible. In the first year of the foundation's existence, we did a Thanksgiving turkey drive at the Church of the Resurrection in Spanish Harlem. And while it certainly did some good—we provided turkeys for seventy-five families, people who otherwise would not have had them—something about it nagged at me for days afterward.

I took some time to think about it, applying curiosity to the task. And what I came to realize was that what we really needed to be doing with the foundation was trying to address the fundamental issues of *why* people couldn't afford to buy a turkey for Thanksgiving in the first place. *That* was what needed addressing. The turkey drive just seemed to me to be a Band-Aid.

And so we shifted the focus of the foundation. We still do the turkey drive—wounds need Band-Aids, after all, to help stop the bleeding. But we now put most of our energies into improving education and finding jobs for people in the community who need them, things that, hopefully, will prevent the wounds from being inflicted in the first place.

Curiosity is about the *why* and the *how*. If we're not asking these questions, the scope of our vision is narrowed. Curiosity expands our minds so we can receive information and really *see* things, and continue to improve ourselves and continue to contribute to society.

Be curious. Open yourself up to receiving information. Lock in on that information with purpose, and then execute it with intention. And then open yourself up for more. Be prepared. Be willing to try. Also, be willing to fail and then learn from that failure.

Another character trait is *awareness*.

The first step, when it comes to this, is to be self-aware, to be aware of where we are, mentally and physically. Being present with ourselves is a huge part of this. So is moving with a purpose and executing with intention. So is validating our progress— that's being aware in real time.

Brené Brown has written and spoken much on the need for self-awareness, especially when it comes to leadership. (We are all leaders, by the way, whether we know it or not. Some of us lead others. All of us lead ourselves. We do this with our words and actions.) Self-awareness, as Brown says, is about managing our own emotions. If we are not self-aware, she says, "we often unknowingly lead from hurt, not heart," which, she continues, "is a huge energy suck" and leads to "distrust and disengagement," for us and everyone around us.

Being self-aware also means being aware of our surroundings, of what's around us. When we are not aware of our surroundings, we become like the person on the highway who drives slowly in the passing lane, unaware that we are slowing everyone else around us down. We are not the only person on this road of life. We always have to check all of our mirrors and pay special attention to our blind spots, both on the road and in life. Are we aware of our own emotions? Are we the ones driving slowly in the passing lane?

In political terms, the word "aware" has been transformed into the word "woke." And because it is a political term, it has become very divisive. At its essence, though, being "woke" simply means being empathetic and sympathetic to other people and their circumstances. But because it's now a political term, we're going to avoid it here and stick with "aware."

Be aware of the Black Lives Matter movement and why it exists. Be aware of the LGBTQ+ community and why it exists. Be aware of the Me Too movement, and not just the bad people who got caught, but the victims. Be aware of people who don't vote for the same political candidates that you do, of both the people who think like you do and the people who do not. Be aware of how we talk to each other, and about each other, in public, on social media.

Awareness is built on the foundation of curiosity. Curiosity provides the knowledge we need to be aware, to be empathetic and sympathetic. Curiosity plus awareness helps us understand one another. Understanding is the first step in turning what would appear to be a hopeless divide into something that can help unite. A high level of curiosity and awareness helps us strive for love and understanding.

I am well aware that not everyone I instruct believes in the same things I do. But the point of my instruction is to get us all to the higher ground, to have us all invest in ourselves—to feel good and look good—so we can reach the summit of doing better, where we are released from the self and become curious, aware, and ready and willing to be empathetic and sympathetic and provide care and love and help to those who need it.

The last characteristic is *rebelliousness*.

As you know, I have been rebellious all of my life. But for the vast majority of that time, I was not very good at it. I didn't put a lot of thought behind my nonconformity. I was merely rebellious for the sake of being rebellious. Getting kicked out of school is not the type of rebelliousness we need to strive for. What I'm talking about is a more calculated rebelliousness.

I'm talking about rebelling against the mindsets that hem us in. An example is what happens in class. On a climb, our bodies and minds are basically screaming at us to quit because of the pain and the work. But we rebel against those thoughts, outwork them, keep pushing, and get better because of it. We feel and see the benefits of that rebelliousness when we get through the workout.

Because, the same thing happens off the bike. When negativity, doubt, fear, or complacency enter our minds, we rebel against them and grow and improve. I rebelled against all of those things when I got the janitor job at Flywheel.

Rebelliousness is about going against the constraints that others have placed in our way, like someone telling us a goal we are shooting for has no chance of being reached. Ruth rebelled against the prevailing thought that women couldn't be disruptors. She proved that was not true. Steph Curry rebelled against the critics that said he didn't belong in the NBA because he was undersize. Four championships later, Steph has silenced every person who doubted him.

Rebelliousness is also about going against the restraints that we have placed in our own way, the rules that we have constructed for ourselves that stall us out. It's about viewing ourselves as who we want to be, not who we used to be. Think we can't reach a goal we've set for ourselves? Try. Fail. Learn. Try again.

All of these characteristics fit together. Curiosity is asking ourselves: "Why has it always been done this way?" Awareness is trying to figure out why people are like they are, about pushing ourselves to understand and be empathetic and sympathetic, about trying to unite instead of taking the easy way out and dividing and remaining unaware. Rebellion is taking those two things and asking ourselves: "Why *can't* we do it?"

When curiosity, awareness, and rebellion align, they conquer negativity and activate our greatness. They get us up the mountain to the top. And, once we've reached the summit, they send us back down, extending our hands out, offering help to others.

PART THREE

DO BETTER

CHAPTER 11

SEEING A LIGHT IN OTHERS

We've taken those steps up the mountain now. Our next step takes us to the summit. Do better.

We don't do better so that we can just make more money or get a promotion at work, though both of those things could very well be the by-products of the process. We don't ascend to the mountaintop so that others can see us. No. We've done all of the work and pushed ourselves to the limit to reach the mountaintop *so that we can see others.*

And we see them so we can help them. After all, we're now equipped to do so. We know what it's like to be at the bottom of the mountain. We know how much grit it takes to climb it.

So we start back down. We look for someone who is at the bottom of the mountain and is afraid to climb, and we help them take that first step. We find someone who is halfway up, and we cheer them along as they keep climbing. We find someone who has taken some steps but has turned around, and we coax them back onto the upward path. We find someone who is near the top but just needs a little nudge to reach the summit. This is where our greatness is fully activated.

The quintessence of doing better is the duty it entails. By choosing empathy over ignorance, courage over fear, and love over hate, we've found that light. We shine that light on others who are shrouded in darkness. We want others to feel like we do as we make the summit, because when we all operate at a higher level, we can build stronger communities, achieve more, collaborate better, and understand and empathize with one another. This is enlightenment. This is the universal force and language known as love. That love is never meant to be kept within. It is meant to be given and shared.

And don't forget: We benefit from this, too. When our families and communities do better, we (personally) do better. Winning with your team is a helluva lot better than just winning by yourself.

The classes I teach are a daily exercise in doing better together, practice for the real world. "Peloton," the actual word, comes from the bike-racing world. A peloton is a group of bikers who ride together during a race to help each other. Riding together in a group conserves energy by reducing air drag. It instills a sense of teamwork and camaraderie. It pushes everyone forward, together. It is a metaphor for love.

Every class I teach goes through a progression. We warm up, start sweating, start moving our minds and bodies, start thinking differently, start viewing the challenge ahead of us as something we can accomplish. We feel good.

We use that energy to tackle a hill. It hurts, but we rebel against that mindset and make it through. We validate that accomplishment. We look good.

And then, once we're there, we look around. We let everyone know that we can see *them*. We send a virtual high five to the people in front of us *and* the people behind us. And on the next hill, we push those people in front of us and help pull up the people behind us. This is how love builds. This is how love spreads.

There's a competitive edge instilled in my classes. This is on purpose. It's done so we will be equipped with a competitive edge in life. But that competitive edge is not about beating the scores of others. It's about pushing ourselves to help push others.

I'm only present in the class to help. The riders do all of the work. I'm the shot of espresso if people need it. I'm there to motivate, to help shine the light. I teach from the side, not from the front or the back. I'm part of the peloton, all of us moving together, as one.

Remember, though, that the destination of our journey is merely the starting point of another journey. There are more summits to climb. Feeling good, looking good, and doing better is a constant and ever-evolving process. We reach the mountaintop, and then we head back down to the bottom, bringing others with us back up. We climb new mountaintops and then head back down again and bring others with us back up. We activate our greatness every single day. We wake up. We hit our free throws. We stay mentally and physically healthy. We check in on ourselves. We check in on our parents and our homies. We do it all at game speed. And every single day, we get a little better at it.

. . .

I was always just OK at math in school, never great at it. I believed that math wasn't that creative and that it lacked movement. Creativity and movement were the ways I learned best back then.

But I was wrong, of course, as I was about a lot of things back in those school days. Math is fundamental. It solves problems. It's a way of seeing how things fit together and what happens *when* those things fit together. It has its own poetry and movement in that it joins ideas in order to express something.

One day at home, I was thinking about something that had come into my head that I'd said out loud in class, something about subtracting doubt and adding courage to our lives. I sat there and jotted down some notes. After a few revisions, I came up with a math equation. This math equation is the central one for feel good, look good, and do better:

> ***Subtract your doubt, add your courage, multiply your hustle, and we divide the love.***

(You'll no doubt notice there are four elements to this equation, not three as in "feel good, look good, do better." I told you I was only OK at math. Let's roll with it.)

This equation, like a lot of math equations, is simple but profound.

We subtract the doubt from our lives because it is our kryptonite. Doubt is our negativity. It holds us back. It stops us from opening those doors of opportunity. Get rid of it.

Once we've removed the doubt that has held us back, we add in something that will open up those doors of opportunity: courage. Courage is what enables us to try, to prepare, to fail, and to learn. Courage allows us to live a life that's authentic to ourselves and not the life that others expect us to live.

Once we get the courage, we find the hustle. Courage is the belief we can do it, and it opens the doors. Hustle is putting that courage to work and actually walking through those doors. For us to be great, though, we can't just hustle. We have to multiply it, or outwork it. We outwork ourselves today to get where we're going tomorrow.

Those three parts of the equation are the feel good and look good stages. They get us to the mountaintop. Once we've joined those first three elements, we've created love, enough of it that we can divide it up and spread it around. In a Peloton class, we divide up—or spread—that love and send it to those behind us and those in front of us. In life, we divide up that love and send it to our families, friends, communities, and the greater world. Dividing our love reinforces the steps we took to get to that moment. It helps us subtract our doubt, add our courage, and multiply our hustle.

This equation is our $E=MC^2$, Einstein's famous equation for how everything in the world fits together. In his equation, energy can become our mass, and mass can become our energy. In our equation, our lives create our energy and our energy creates our lives. This is our equation for life. It's also the formula for helping us see the light in others.

• • •

In my first two-plus years of my career at Peloton, things just *moved*. The company was growing so fast that we could all barely keep up. We went to the Consumer Electronics Show in Las Vegas—the biggest tech and entertainment convention in the world—and felt like the belles at the ball with all of the attention. New instructors were hired nearly every month because of increased demand. My live classes went from five thousand riders, to ten thousand, to fifteen thousand.

I was having a great time. There were regular shoots for ads featuring instructors that appeared on TV and the Internet, which made us all feel like rock stars. The *New York Times* wrote two big stories about us, both of which mentioned me. I traveled all over—Greece, St. Barts, Italy, Costa Rica, Hawaii. I jumped out of an airplane for the first time. I got a new apartment in Hudson Yards. I rode helicopters from the city to East Hampton. I bought my first car, a white Mercedes 250 Class, as a sort of replacement for that car that had been stolen when I was in college.

When it came to work, though, I still hustled. I still treated every class like it was an audition and was still scared to death of missing one and potentially missing out on an opportunity. For motivation, I kept my failures in the back of my mind but not so close that they would get in the way.

It is perfectly OK for us to enjoy life, especially when we've earned it. But when things are rolling great, it's also time to be a bit careful and remember those steps we must take every day up the mountain.

I wasn't being careful enough. With things so crazy and fast, I started skipping some essential steps that got me to where I was. I took my eye off of the ball a bit.

But then I was thrown back abruptly into the present.

•　•　•

You'll remember that the proverbial straw that broke the camel's back for me at military school—the episode that ultimately led to my dismissal—was when my maternal grandfather died, and the school leaders wouldn't let me go to the funeral.

His wife, my grandmother—who we called Pome—lived on after he died. She was a huge part of my life. She showered me with easy love, an important counterweight to the tough love dished out by my parents. She visited us from Haiti a number of times when I was growing up, and even lived with us for a short time. I was young, so I didn't quite understand then how she was the living testament to the space and time traveled by my mom and our family.

In September 2018, two years and eight months into my Peloton life and right in the midst of the craziness—she died. Her death hit me very hard. And it shocked me back into reality. I realized that I had lost touch with myself, that I was moving so fast all of the time that I was not making the time to take a breath and be present with myself. I was rushing through my morning routine and sometimes even failing to make my bed. I was enjoying life, but I wasn't really pausing to take the time to validate my experiences. Instead, I pushed them aside in a frantic search for the next one. And because I wasn't pausing to validate and process anything, I wasn't learning. Even though it appeared that I was living the best life, I was, in fact, really just existing. Yes, it is possible to exist and not live even when things are going great.

I wasn't going to miss *this* funeral for anything.

I flew to Haiti with my mom. I hadn't been down there since I was a kid, so she took me around and reintroduced me to cousins and friends of our family whom I had met when I was too young to remember. She showed me around town, taking me to places where she had hung out when growing up there, places that were important to the story of our family. I made sure to listen—really listen—to what she had to say and speak very little.

One hot morning when I was down there, I sat up on the roof of Pome's house. I was surrounded by my uncle and some cousins, and I listened to my uncle talk about Haiti, about our roots. My cousins and I asked him questions. It was quiet, those few hours in the morning before the real heat hits, and the only sound in the world seemed to be our voices. And for the first time as an adult, I started to understand where my family and I came from, and why it mattered. America was my home, where the family tree grew. But this is where the seed had been planted and the roots remained. I came to realize and appreciate—for the first time—the interconnectedness among the generations. I understood what the sacrifices of previous generations meant for all of us. Our grandparents crawled so our parents could walk. Our parents walked so we could run. And we run so that future generations can sprint. We have an obligation to honor all of the sacrifices that led to us. *If we truly understand where we come from, we understand how far we can—and must—take it.*

Pome was the reason I figured out what it really meant to do better. She always told me "the key to life is giving." She spent her life giving to her children and grandchildren. She told me that selfish people are usually unhappy people, and that unselfish people are usually happy. Unselfishness, she said, was the highest state of being and made life fulfilling.

We would all lead more fulfilling lives if we understood this about unselfishness and giving. And practiced it. It's not necessarily about giving money to good causes, though that's certainly a very good thing to do. It's more about giving guidance, inspiration, confidence, and love. Those things are more valuable than money. Anybody can give you money. But if someone guides or inspires you or gives you confidence or love? That's a higher form of currency.

Even in the midst of moving too fast in my life, I was still practicing "do better." I was sharing and spreading love to my riders and the people in my life. But Pome's death changed something for me. It made me realize that there's an entire new level to all of this, that there was another summit for me with a broader view that was more present and more authentic.

And I realized that this summit would remain out of reach for me unless I changed. I had to transform myself into something that I had never been in my life. I realized that the shell I had constructed around myself during my childhood, which helped protect me, was maybe a little too well built. I would still need it—protecting ourselves and our energy is still vital. But I realized that I needed to open it up a little more, maybe even a lot more. I realized that I needed to make myself vulnerable.

Vulnerability can be a taboo subject, particularly among men and even more so among Black men. It was a taboo subject in my family, for sure. My dad came from that paternalistic Haitian culture, where a man had to be a man and not show any supposed weakness. I had observed him closely when he was sick. I had seen how stone cold he was about the whole thing, and I realized now, in retrospect, how much that had eaten at him and damaged him.

But being vulnerable is a must. It's the key to opening up another, higher dimension of ourselves. Vulnerability isn't a weakness. It's our power. A big part of doing better and activating our greatness is the ability to be vulnerable. It's hard to do—we have to rebel against being comfortable and, if you're a man, rebel against a stigma. But it's a necessary act to open up our world.

To that point, I had been turning my pain into power, but doing so mainly internally, using it as a way to motivate me to motivate others. I wasn't making myself vulnerable to anyone but myself.

But after Pome died, I started to tap into my pain, and instead of keeping it to myself, I shared it with others, by speaking about it openly. I talked about my failures, my dad, about what I was going through at any given moment. In one class after Pome died, I broke down crying, pedaling through my emotions, something I never would have done before. That shell wouldn't have allowed it.

After that class, I received dozens of emails, direct messages, and even letters, mostly from other men. They told me that by allowing myself to be vulnerable, I'd helped them see it was OK for them to do it, as well.

Showing and sharing my vulnerability helped me break out of a box I had trapped myself in. From that point on, the entire ridership and every class became more engaged and loving. Vulnerability unlocked that.

The ability to be vulnerable is extremely important for our own sake, for our growth and evolution. But it is, perhaps, even more important for what it allows us to do for others. Being vulnerable improves how we do better by opening us up to being able to *see the light in others that they don't see themselves*.

We can be that person who believes in someone else who needs believing in. We can be that person who instills confidence in the person who needs it. We can be that person who loves the person who needs that love.

Everyone has that light. Some people view it as hope at the end of the tunnel. Some people view it as an oncoming train. Our job is to help them see it as the former. We do this by being curious, aware, empathetic, and being open to the possibility that everyone has some good within them. We do this, ultimately, by finding our own light. If we see our own light, it can help lead us to the light found in others.

I try not to just preach this mantra, but exemplify it. When I'm on the bike, my duty is to see the light in those people who are riding with me. I try to do the same off the bike. I've been down in those dark places where no one understands you. I look for the light in people who are in that space, the light that will help them get out of it.

I'll put it this way: Whether I'm on or off the bike, I want to be to everyone else what Ruth was to me.

• • •

Angels, man. I think about them often. By "angels," I mean the people in our lives who were there for us when we needed it, just out of the goodness of their hearts and almost as if they were assigned to us. The people who saw the light in us when everything in our world was so dark that we were blind to it. They are the people who were in the seats in the theater who we finally saw when the lights came on.

Ruth was an obvious angel for me. She saw some light in me that I didn't even know existed and gave me confidence that I was great even when I didn't believe it. But there have been plenty of others. My kindergarten teacher, Susan Verde, Coach Hartwell, and my middle school counselor certainly were. (Our teachers and educators, my mom among them, are truly our essential workers in life.) So, too, were Captain Ragsdale, Jerome and his family, and Jayvee. All of these people selflessly helped me when I needed it most, asking for nothing in return, the highest form of unselfishness and character. Character, as they say, is how you treat people who can do nothing for you.

My greatest angel, though, was my mom. Despite all of the hardships, despite all of my self-inflicted wounds, she was always there. She wasn't the light at the end of the tunnel—her energy and love lit the entire tunnel up. Though her efforts were often hampered by my dad (and by me), she never gave up on me, which was the only thing that made it possible for me to never completely give up on myself. Her love was unconditional, and that unconditional love was what allowed me to never let the darkness fully envelope me. (Parents out there, I implore you: Never, ever, give up on your kids. Whether you know it or not, you *are* that light at the end of the tunnel.)

We all have these angels in our lives. Acknowledging and embracing our own vulnerability allows us to better receive them, to see them for who they are. More important: Vulnerability allows *us* to see ourselves as they see us. That greatness within.

I wasn't ready to receive most of my angels when they found me. I was young and too wrapped up in my own darkness. But I see them now. I've seen them ever since those theater lights went on. And I'm ready and more open to receive any new ones who come along now.

When we discover an angel, we should accept them. And then thank and praise them. Because what they have done for us opens a door for us to go do the same for others. It allows *us* to become angels, to look for that light in others, that greatness, and help activate it. To walk back down that mountain and bring someone back up with us. To carry them if we have to. And to do it all with no obligation.

This is what doing better is all about.

CHAPTER 12

CAN'T QUARANTINE THE HUSTLE

Life is chaotic. Life throws shit at us. Change happens. We lose a job. We lose a friend. We miss our flight. Our kids get sick. We get sick. Our dog poops on the floor.

And this is when we need to be innovative and flexible. This is when we need to adapt and adjust to change.

So, how do we do this? We first must take some time to think, to make a game plan. We need to lay out our own version of the Serenity Prayer—to figure out which things we *can* control, and which things we *cannot*. We focus on the former. The rest is just noise.

We can control our thoughts and habits. We can concentrate on the positive. For many of us, the early part of the pandemic meant being shut in with just our families. This was frustrating, of course. No one likes to be shut in. But the people who handled this the best were the ones who saw this as an opportunity to lean in to that forced family time, to make it special as opposed to a hassle. Missed your flight and stuck in an airport in a foreign city for twenty-four hours? Don't sulk. Make the most of it and get out and explore that city.

Another way to manage change and chaos is to think about goals, but to do it in the right way. I like to use what's known as the SMART criteria. (I use this for goal setting in nonchaotic times, too.) SMART is an acronym for the types of goals we should strive to set: Specific, Measurable, Achievable, Realistic, and Timely.

The corporate world has kind of co-opted this idea. It was presented as a guide in business for managers to evaluate and assist their employees. But we shouldn't just leave this to the business world, because it applies to all types of goal setting. And, in the end, we are all the managers of the most important person: ourselves. I use this for goals when it comes to family, friends, work, and finances. It lays out a clear road map.

We should also reach back to our strengths in times of change. Are you a good communicator? Talk to people. Good at mentoring? Find someone who needs help, or apply those skills to yourself. Creative? A problem solver? A fixer? A negotiator? Use it all.

Use the change as an excuse to experiment. Use your curiosity and open up your mindset to *see* things you haven't seen and then see where they take you. Try something new. During the pandemic, thousands of people tried new sports—tennis, running, yoga, fishing, skiing—and got hooked. People started cooking dishes they never had before and gardening and finally getting around to doing house renovations.

Change is what we're preparing for when we add resistance to our rides and our lives. It's how we teach ourselves to become comfortable with the uncomfortable.

Steve Jobs famously got fired from Apple, the company he cofounded. But instead of just throwing his hands up in the air and giving up, he went even harder. He founded another computer company *and* the company that would eventually become Pixar. Twelve years later, he took over Apple again as it was about to go bankrupt and guided it to become the company it is today.

We write our own life story. Never let change become an excuse. And never let it stifle your hustle.

• • •

It's important for us to realize that everything we do and have done in our lives can come into play to help us in a moment when we need it, and especially in moments of change or chaos. Yes, we can turn our past pain into present and future power. But we can also find strength in the everyday things we do, those little things that become our thoughts, habits, and priorities. There is a lot of power to be found there, too. We just need to open ourselves up, to allow them to help us, and be innovative and flexible. And we can't make excuses that let them slip away—even if we have an excuse that's easily found. . . .

• • •

It's April 24, 2020. Like much of the country—and the world—I am in my living room. Stuck. My new apartment is in Manhattan, near Peloton's brand-new Hudson Yards studios, which, like the rest of the city and most of the world, has been closed down for a few weeks now. I'm getting acquainted with my new four walls. A bit too acquainted.

The shut-down city's eerie quiet is shattered every few minutes with the sound of sirens. I can see Thirty-Fourth Street and Penn Station through my window. They are utterly empty and quiet, like those unnerving scenes in the movie *I Am Legend*. At night, the red lights of ambulances sneak through the cracks in my curtains and dance on my ceiling as I fall into a restless sleep. There's a virus out there, a pandemic that has swept from the eastern part of the globe through Europe and is now ripping through New York City and beginning to tear through the rest of the country. People are scared of both the known and the unknown. People are just scared, period. We've never faced anything like this before.

So, yes, I am in my living room. Only today, it's different. Today, I am sitting in the saddle of my bike. There's a piece of masking tape that I've put down on my floor that marks the spot where the camera's tripod stands. That's my couch in the camera's viewfinder. That's my basketball and my plant over there. That's my window behind me.

Right now, I am an experiment. When the Peloton studios shut down a few weeks ago, it meant the end of live classes. Riders could still do workouts, of course, but they had to rely on the old classes that had been recorded. Those recorded classes were plenty good and came in handy, especially during this unique time. There were hundreds, if not thousands, of hours of fitness content on the Peloton app. But there is nothing like the live classes, nothing like being there in the moment with an instructor and other riders.

Peloton knew this. The old recorded classes would hold riders' attention for a bit, but the company felt it needed to try to be pro-active during the pandemic and not just sit back and let *it* dictate what happened. So they asked me if I would try something. The idea was to start doing live classes again, but not from the shut-down studios. They'd be done from the instructors' homes. And they asked if I'd be willing to do the first one.

My answer, like the one I gave when offered the job as a jan-itor at Flywheel: a simple "hell, yes." I would get a camera and a tripod and some sound and lighting equipment delivered, but because of the pandemic restrictions, Peloton would not be able to send anyone over to help, no producers or studio managers. We were going to do it all remotely. So I asked my great friend and business partner, Dave, to help me. We'd basically been limiting our social interactions to just each other since the beginning of the shutdown, anyway.

I was flattered and honored to be one of the first instructors to be asked to do what would become known as "Live from Home." The team at Peloton had demonstrated faith in me and trusted me to get the job done. I wanted to reciprocate that faith and trust and rise to the occasion and the challenge. My mindset wasn't to play it safe and just try to get a base hit. I wanted to knock this opportunity out of the park.

I prepared for that class like I always did, but with even more attention to the finer details because I was *really* on my own now. Dave was there to help me set up the equipment and the light-ing. He also helped watch my puppy (I only had one at the time) and monitor the Google Hangouts chat with the producers from behind the camera. But everything else was up to me. I had to cut the music. I had to direct the camera shot.

I set up my playlist, memorizing the songs down to the time codes. I wanted it to be a fun ride. We would do some real work on some challenging hills. But I also wanted to leave ample time for some reflection and validation along the way.

At 9:30 in the morning, the red light came on and we started to roll, with Dave behind the tripod, making sure the camera stayed on point. The music began to play.

"My kings and queens," I said into the camera. "Thank you for showing up today. On every pedal stroke, I will have your back . . . I see you. Let's do this."

And off we went, twenty-two thousand riders and me, together in my crib.

The first five minutes of the class went smoothly. In fact, it was better than smooth. We were rocking. It felt great to be back on the bike, instructing.

And then, suddenly and without any warning, my headphones conked out. No music came through. I knew something could easily go wrong during this first ride, but I didn't think it would be the music, which is probably the most important component of the ride for the instructor, as you know. My computer was still working, so all of the riders could still hear the music. But I couldn't.

When I watched that ride later on, I saw a small look of concern on my brow at the moment that the music went out. Not panic. But concern. I shot a little glance Dave's way. He didn't immediately understand what had happened. And I couldn't just stop the live class. I signaled a few times to my ears, and he caught on and frantically looked around my apartment for an extra set of earphones. I had several loose AirPods and cases lying around on my desk—all malfunctioning for some reason or another—but he finally found an alternate pair that actually worked, crawled up to get as close, but not so close that he would get in the camera's shot, and tossed them to me (it was a great toss, by the way). I'm still riding at this point, still instructing—and I catch them flawlessly, without missing a pedal stroke. *Ah, we're in the clear,* I thought.

But when I tried them, they didn't work, either. It hit me then that something was wrong with the feed, and not the earphones themselves. If this was going to work, I had to assume there would be no more music for me to hear and that I would have to instruct without it.

I took a quick deep breath, inhaling my confidence, exhaling my doubt. I thought about my dad, of course, and his mantra about being prepared. And I also thought about Kobe Bryant and what he did with the game on the line, how he always embraced the challenge and never shied away from it. He was asked once how he felt when the opposing coach sent two players out to guard him. He replied that he would yell to that coach and beg him to put one more defender on him. ("You gotta send another one!" he said.) That was my mindset.

"I got no music, Peloton, but I'm still working," I said to the class. "We're not perfect, but we're still working."

I could see the songs on my laptop monitor and their time codes. That helped because the transitions between songs are pivotal points in the class for an instructor. I also knew the music by heart, knew when the beat dropped and when it picked up, knew when the chorus was coming in and when each verse was done, knew all the intros and the outros. Man, if there was ever a time where being an absolute music fanatic paid off, it was now.

"We have to work against the resistance, Peloton," I said. Usually when I said that, I meant the resistance that the class applied to the ride, with the turn of a knob on the bike that made pedaling harder. But this phrase had taken on a new meaning for me.

And we made it through the rest of the ride. When the camera cut, I was initially livid that we'd had technical difficulties, that it had happened on my biggest stage. But that feeling was quickly overridden by the joy of overcoming that obstacle. My producers on the Google Hangouts literally couldn't believe what had just happened.

Afterward, I discovered that most people on the ride didn't even really register that we'd had technical difficulties at all. It hadn't been perfect, but we got "Live from Home" launched. It would turn out to be a significant part of Peloton's incredible run of success during the pandemic. And it helped hundreds of thousands of people stay sane during an insane time.

• • •

When I was young, my dad always told me that I had an excuse for everything—the bus was late, I didn't have time to do my homework, that teacher I had talked back to had started it, etc. And he was correct. I bullshitted my way through life back then.

I've thought about that time of my life and all of the excuses I made for myself. I could have done it all better. I could have taken control of the situation and changed my actions. That would have allowed me some room to find success. In order to find success, we need to be proactive, to look for solutions and not just an easy way out. It requires *less excuses, more adjustments*.

That phrase popped into my head when the music went out during that first class from home. In fact, I said it out loud at one point. It would have been totally excusable just to tell people that the ride was over because I couldn't hear anything, that this was our first attempt, that we'd get better, that there was a pandemic going on. And so on and so on. Excuses were everywhere if I wanted them. The riders probably would have been OK with it, too, given the circumstances. It was an experiment, after all. Scrap the idea. Wait until the studios reopen.

But nah—it was an opportunity to show myself, my company, and the world that there're levels to this shit. I knew I had put in the work. The work that no one sees. I wouldn't have been OK with making excuses. Not now. Not anymore. So I stayed calm and looked for the adjustment.

I thought about my dad, too, at that moment, because everything starts with preparation. I had no idea that the music was going to cut out, but I knew that something could happen. I was prepared for that and, thus, prepared not to fail.

I didn't realize it at the time, but I had been preparing for this moment for the last five years of my life, with every free throw that I'd made. The A/V training in college. All of those small moments at Flywheel. All of those Peloton classes and the work I had put in before and after them. We all have these little things we've done or learned in the past that can help us in the present and future.

I felt like I had no room for excuses because Peloton had entrusted me to do that first "Live from Home" class. I knew that John Foley and others at Peloton were watching. I wanted to prove that we, as a company, could thrive during these uncertain times and not just fold up the tents. I wanted to prove that *I* could thrive, too, no matter what obstacles were put in my path. I felt like my character would be determined in that moment, based on whether I made an excuse or made an adjustment.

There was also no room for excuses because of the broader implications of "Live from Home." This wasn't just about the company or me. Live classes at that time meant something else entirely. We were all scared and paralyzed a bit by the pandemic. Yes, I wanted and needed to get back on the bike for myself, for sure. But more than that, I thought I could help—help people move their bodies when they were stuck inside their homes, and help people move their minds when they were stuck inside their heads.

"Live from Home" would, in the end, force me to become a better instructor and motivator. It was comfortable to lead classes from Peloton's studios. There, I have a full team, with producers and tech people, with multiple cameras and perfect lighting.

Teaching from home allowed me to be more real. I was teaching from the comfort of my living room. What better arena to show my game than the place where I practiced every single day? Thousands of riders coming through *my* front door. (My biggest

"Live from Home" class was, in fact, thirty-six thousand riders.) It was truly, authentically, me. The lighting was far from perfect, but it worked. There was one camera, which meant less motion than a class shot from the studio. Within those constraints, I had to figure out how to keep the class moving, how to keep people motivated without all of the crutches I had in the studio.

I did that by tapping more deeply into my emotions. I stared at the couch in my apartment and saw myself as a young man, so depressed that I couldn't get off it. And then I saw the transformation, when I got motivated and overcame the depression and got up off that couch. I channeled all of those emotions into my rides.

My goal—my duty, really—was to make sure that no one in my class, especially during this scary, draining time, would be left behind, unable to get up off the couch.

• • •

During the early stages of the pandemic, certain words entered our everyday vocabulary—"isolation," "social distancing," "community spread," "quarantine."

While none of those words had happy vibes, it was the last one that really bothered me. It just felt so . . . confining. I decided to turn it on its head, and help people use it in a way that wasn't confining, but in a way that could help us shake free of its constraints. I came up with this phrase: *Can't quarantine the hustle*.

During that early part of the pandemic, when we were locked down, there were a lot of people who retreated into shells. But I didn't want to do that and I didn't want any of my riders to do it, either. We had a choice: BS our way through this, or get proactive and give ourselves the chance to come out of it better than we were when we went into it.

The lockdown and quarantines didn't mean we had to come to a full stop. It didn't mean we couldn't still hustle. In fact, it was the opposite. It was precisely the time when we could show ourselves and the world what we were capable of doing. It was an opportunity. We were fortunate to be alive. We owed it not only to ourselves, but also to the people who were sick or who had died to live through this and not just exist through it. Every single day, we are blessed to have two things: a chance and a choice. And the choices we make that day determine the chances we get.

The hustle is how we operate in life. It's how we find the motivation and discipline to innovate, and then what we do with those new muscles we've grown. It's how we don't seek out excuses and look instead for adjustments.

This phrase has a greater resonance than COVID. It applies to our lives and the things that happen to us, both big and small, that threaten to confine us. Instead of cowering in the face of those threats, we have to take the opportunity to hustle, create, prosper, and grow. We can't let these things box us, or our vision, in. None of the obstacles set in our way can stop us. When faced with them, we use our motivation and then tap into our discipline when that motivation runs low. We don't quit. Our hustle can't be quarantined.

That hustle is about the love we talked about earlier, too. We can't quarantine that, either. Hustling is about growing, nurturing, and ultimately sharing love. My goal with my classes—and this book and in life—is to help people acquire the tools needed to take our love out of quarantine. Because, unlike COVID, love is something we *want* to spread. When we finish a class or a task, or reach a goal, we feel good and look good, and we want to share that feeling—that light—and free it from quarantine. Maybe we proceed to call a friend who we haven't talked to in a while, just to check in. They feel the love when we do this. We've spread the love to them and, in doing so, we've made it much more likely that our friend will spread the love herself to someone else. That's the butterfly effect. That's the community spread of love. That's the innovation, the creativity, the flexibility, the hustle. That's at the heart of doing better.

CHAPTER 13

IT'S NOT ABOUT ME, IT'S ABOUT WE

We should all think of ourselves as planters. Every day, we can plant little seeds of kindness in others, seeds that will, with care and light that we shine, activate and grow the kindness of the community around us and, eventually, the kindness of the communities around ours.

Robin Arzón was the first "planter" I met at Peloton. She changed me literally from the minute I saw her in that first ad during that NBA playoff game. She is a goddess, mentor, and sister to me. She is the daughter of two immigrants, and was one of the few people of color in a leadership position at the company when I joined. After a traumatic experience, she changed her life—she left her comfortable job in law to pursue her passion, athletics, and landed at Peloton.

All of this was very inspiring, of course, but it was the way in which she openly shared and shined her light on others that was so cool. She showed me what it was like to be an instructor and how to make it something more than that—a business. She always had my back. And she reinforced what John Foley had told me when I started: Be yourself. In fact, when she said it, it was more emphatic. John told me to be myself. Robin showed me how.

As I mentioned, I first came into Peloton as a hothead, looking to show everyone how successful I could be. Over time, Robin, Tunde, Cody, and all the other instructors taught me that it was really about something else. The "Together we go far" motto of the company is not just for show. With the help of the other instructors, I learned that my individual success means nothing if the team is not successful together. This applies to families, friends, and the corporate environment. Success doesn't mean outshining others. It means lifting them up. That's the *do better* part. We all boost each other. We take each other's classes and talk each other up on social media.

We are all different, of course. We all follow the mantra of "Be yourself." But teams can be effective even if there are differences. In fact, they can be more effective. The instructors at Peloton have different strengths and weaknesses. We reach different demographics. What I don't have, Robin and Tunde might. Cody and Ally might lack something that I have. As long as we are all real with each other and realize that we all have an individual greatness, and realize that we all have the same goal, it works. It all works if we do it together. When we start up that mountain, we don't walk five yards apart. We go hand in hand. Same when we come back down, looking for others to help.

In the song "Middle Child," J. Cole talks about success and how useless it is if those around us don't find it, too. What good is it if we're the only one winning and no one else is? Being on the mountaintop by ourselves is lonely. Seeing the people we love and support and trust winning is what it's all about.

. . .

One of the keys to doing better—thus, one of the keys to life—is the people we surround ourselves with. It's so important to surround ourselves with people who believe in us and our vision and who are good, caring, loving, and honest. Authenticity is the key here. If we're authentic, we will naturally surround ourselves with authentic people. And they will become our peloton—they will help us move forward, and we will help them do the same. They are our support system. When we set our goals, it's important to not tell just *anyone* about them—tell the people who will assist you and not dismiss you. The assisters are in your peloton.

The people in my peloton are my family—my mom, my brothers, my aunts and uncles and cousins and, yes, now even my dad. They are Dave and Archie, my best friends and business managers. They are the people I work with at Peloton, like my producer, Shakah Herrera, and my fellow instructors. They are the riders who come to my classes, too, in a broader sense.

When we start to do better in life, we start to create a community, with our thoughts, words, and deeds. Everything is self-reinforcing. We help motivate others when they need it. They help motivate us when we need it. When we win, everyone around us wins. When someone in our peloton wins, we win, too.

The people we surround ourselves with are also part of our discipline. They hold us accountable. We hold them accountable.

We all check each other's egos. They look out for our blind spots. We can plug into them when we need a backup generator for our motivation, and they can do the same with us.

We are each other's safety net in this way. There are times when we all need help getting up the mountain. We won't always be on top mentally, physically, or financially. Our surrounding cast can help get our asses back up when we fall. In the words of Jay-Z in his song "Feelin' It," "Nobody will fall 'cause everyone will be each other's crutches."

There is strength in our peloton. And there is room in our peloton for more than just the people we know. There is also room for stories.

· · ·

Remember back to when you were a kid and you had heroes, people who you never met but who inspired you? Maybe they were famous for whatever reason. Maybe they were even fictional characters in a movie or a book.

I think it's a good thing to keep some of that childlike wonder in our lives and have people in our lives—even people we don't know—who inspire us. This may seem naïve to some—when we get older, we're supposed to drop these types of things, especially when we realize that all people, even our childhood heroes, have flaws.

But heroes are, in the end, really just stories. And stories help create our lives—the stories we tell about ourselves, the stories we have about others in the world. We can take lessons and stories from people we don't even know and adapt them to our own lives. And they can be as motivating and inspirational as anything else in life.

As you undoubtedly can tell by now, I love music. And one of my favorite musicians of all time is a person I have mentioned many times already, a man named Shawn Carter. Or, as he is more commonly known, Jay-Z.

I have never met Jay-Z, but I have listened to his music all of my life and I have studied his story. In that story, I have found some things that we share, and I've found much wisdom. Jay-Z's story, in a way, is its own version of feel good, look good, do better.

Jay-Z had a rough childhood, growing up in the projects. He was eleven years old when his father abandoned his family.

That act thrust Jay-Z into the family leadership role, which meant that he became the provider, even though he was still in middle school. To do that, he entered into what was the easiest and most financially lucrative trade for young Black men at the time in Brooklyn: He started selling crack, something he has said he regrets.

Jay-Z, too, had an angel, a high school teacher who noticed him and how much he loved words and who told him he was special, which no one else ever had.

He's proven her correct. I remember listening to his first album, which came out in 1996. My brothers and their friends listened to it all of the time. I was far too young to fully appreciate the music, but I do remember the way it made me feel when I listened to it: This guy was different.

It is difficult for me to put into words exactly what Jay-Z would come to mean to me as I was growing up, and means to me even now. Though there are many Black role models these days, they still aren't as numerous as they could be. Jay-Z is by no means perfect, but as I got older, I realized that no one was, and that people don't have to be perfect to be good role models. The entire sum of a life—the circumstances, the progress, the desire and attempt and success at making good—must be considered before any verdict is rendered.

One of the things that attracted me to Jay-Z was his ability to turn his pain into power, to give it a voice and use it in a productive manner. He used his childhood, the destitution he grew up in, the trade he was pretty much forced into, and the young lives he saw wasted on the streets to create a narrative to his music. Though our backgrounds are very different—I was very privileged compared to him—all of that resonated with me and inspired me.

It inspired me because he was rapping the truth. The thing about rap that some people—mainly, the people who don't listen to it—don't understand is that it is an art form, representative of the artist's reality. It interprets and reflects within the stories it tells. In any art, language is used as a means to an end, and Jay-Z's sometimes risqué and violent lyrics in his songs are that means. I've always found it strange that some of the same people who consider the movies *The Godfather* and *Scarface* to be classic examples of art—even with their misogyny and violence—do not view the rap of Jay-Z and some of the other best rappers in the same manner.

I think about Jay-Z a lot when I work on my classes, and not just because I frequently use his music. His lyrics, the cadence of his voice, and the beats he has concocted reach us at an emotional level and get us to move our minds, spirits, souls, and bodies. Everything is authentic, and because of that, it connects.

I love the themes of his songs, too, what he preaches: About taking chances to get more out of life. About identifying with truth and not trends. About how other people project their fears, limitations, and shortcomings on us. About how strong belief insulates us from the distracting outside noise.

Jay-Z grew his brand and became a successful CEO. But more than all of that, what has inspired me most about Jay-Z is that he always made it a priority to help others, to do better. Through his record label, he has launched the careers of Rihanna and J. Cole, among others. He forgave his father and reconciled with him shortly before his father died in 2003, which was a ges ture I paid particular attention to. He started a foundation with his mother, which helps kids from disadvantaged backgrounds go to college. "If you can dream it, you can achieve it," he says is the idea behind the foundation, which aims to help people avoid what he went through when he was a kid, to provide them with the opportunities that he did not have. As he wrote in one of his songs, he went through all of his hardships—the poverty, the drug-dealing—"HOV did that / so hopefully you won't have to go through that." His foundation shines a light on others.

What also sets Jay-Z apart from other celebrities, for me any-way, is his willingness to share his life story and everything he has learned. He is putting people on game—helping other people to win. He's used his platform to take his life to an entire new trajectory, and to take and inspire others, like me, along the way.

There's a quote that I love that's been attributed to Malcolm X. It reads: "When 'I' is replaced with 'we,' even 'illness' becomes 'wellness.'" In a sense, what Jay-Z has done is taken the "I" out of the equation.

This is also what Jay-Z has done with the community he has built around him. He's at the center of it in many respects, of course. But it's not about him.

This is what happens when we do better. Our community is premised on the following: *It's not about me, it's about we*.

This is an idea that was first instilled in me during military school. It's the very basis of military training, that whatever one person does affects everyone else, that we work together as a unit to accomplish our goals, and that no person is ever left behind.

That idea was reinforced when I first got on the bike at Flywheel, with Ruth's mantra that classes were to be about the riders and not the instructors. While I do draw from my own experiences when I instruct, I do it with a greater goal in mind. I'm preaching "we," not "me."

And it was all reinforced even more at Peloton, with the general vibe that we are all in this together and that we can only go so far by ourselves, but can go much farther together.

There's a larger resonance to this, as well. "We" allows us to connect with not just our immediate community. It also helps our community understand and connect with other communities, too. It ties into the importance of having awareness and curiosity, of trying to understand where different people are coming from and wanting to seek common ground.

Yes, we all have differences. But those differences are all part of our strength, and they can add to our bonds if they are appreciated, and become valued as bridges and not moats.

It's all about the butterfly effect. Look at the state of our national politics, for instance. It appears broken. Our differences seem irreconcilable. But they aren't. The very perception that they are, though, is damaging.

We can help change all of that. How we do that is to start locally, on the most granular level that there is: with ourselves. We practice gratitude. We become trustworthy, honest, unselfish, and loving. We spread those vibes and, in doing so, create a community of "we" around us, based on those vibes. We stay curious and see other people and other communities not as "other," but as "we," and aim to bring them into the fold, just as we do with the individuals in our community. By doing that, we can begin to stitch those communities together into a greater whole.

It starts with the little things. We say "good morning" to the people we see on the street and in the grocery store, and we smile as we say it.

Acts of kindness, big or small. Practice them. Kindness is our legacy. At our funerals, people won't be talking about our accomplishments. They'll be talking about what kind of person we were. Make sure they have a lot to say. Kindness is the kindling for the fire. This kindling happens person-to-person and then happens community-to-community.

• • •

There is one thing to remember about doing better and building our peloton and our community that is vitally important: It requires that we always pour from a full cup. We function at our best—as individuals and as positive contributors to our communities—when our cup is full. When our cup is drained, so are we, and we lose the ability to love and be kind and do better.

One way we keep our cups full every day is to keep working on feeling good and looking good. We should never neglect ourselves. Maintain good discipline and maintain that good selfishness. We do this for ourselves and for the sake of others.

When we feel like our cup is getting close to empty, there is something important that we need to do: We have to ***disconnect to reconnect***.

The job. The kids. The mortgage. The relentlessness of life. We all get to a point sometimes when we need to recharge. If we don't recharge, we burn out. We shut down mentally and retreat into a cocoon. And when that happens, we can't help anyone else—or ourselves.

The communities we build through doing better need to be cared for, and that starts with us. One way to look at this: The community we have built is like a string of those old-school Christmas tree lights, the ones that ran on one shared series circuit. We are all bulbs on that string. The light from that string shines brightly when everything is charged, when all bulbs are in working order. But if one bulb starts to go dim or conks out, it affects every other bulb on the string. Sometimes, *we* are that bulb that's going dim. And that's when it's time to address it. Disconnect. Recharge. And then reconnect.

In an ideal world, disconnecting can happen on a vacation, one that we *really* take, when we really leave everything behind. If this is a possibility for us, great. Go on that vacation. Don't work. Don't even think about work. Think only about ourself. We'll address everything that needs addressing when we get back home.

But we don't live in an ideal world, so fully getting away is not always possible, if it's possible at all. Many of us can't take a "real" vacation these days, not with our present state of constant connectivity. But that's OK. We can still disconnect enough to get a full recharge. If we have to work a bit while on vacation, do it. But in those spaces of time when we do not have to work, don't! Step away from the computer and the phone. Go for a walk. Sit outside. Stare at nothing. Daydream.

Disconnecting doesn't have to be saved just for vacations, though. Those happen far too infrequently, anyway. We can—and should—find time to disconnect every weekend. Take a brief pause from social media. Watch a movie. Go see a friend. Work out. Spend time with our family and friends. Do something creative. Volunteer in our community. Don't worry. The phone and social media, like our work, will be there when we're done disconnecting. I promise.

Given the amount of time we work and are connected to our devices, it's also important to find time to disconnect every single day. Maybe we have only ten minutes to do so? That's OK. Take that time. Disconnect. Recharge.

Disconnecting is so vital these days, when our phone, with all of its distractions and neediness, is always in our hands or pockets. It keeps us in a state of always being "on." And we just can't function that way, not for long, anyway, if we're always plugged in.

The goal, in the end, is not just to operate with a full cup. That cup should be overfilled in order for us to be our best—for ourselves and for others.

CHAPTER 14

I CAN'T BREATHE

In early 2020, I moved into my new apartment in Hudson Yards. I finally had a place of my own. I liked the responsibility and I liked not having weird roommates anymore.

Peloton continued to grow like crazy and so did my classes. The average weekly ridership for my classes grew into the hundreds of thousands. That was a hard number for me to process until Dave put it into a visual perspective for me one day. "AT, you're basically filling up Madison Square Garden in each of these live rides," he said. It was a trip.

Things were really rocking . . . until the pandemic hit that year and everything shut down. So "Live from Home" was a godsend, for me and for my riders. It offered us all a way to stay strong and sharp, a way to work together to move our minds and bodies and to get by, one day at a time.

I noticed during that time that more and more professional athletes were riding with me in my classes—they were just as stir-crazy as the rest of us and were looking to maintain their competitive edge. Tennis legend Roger Federer started doing some rides. So did NFL quarterback Patrick Mahomes. The NBA's Golden State Warriors did some classes as a team-bonding exercise. Even PGA Tour golfers got into the mix. Rory McIlroy and Justin Thomas were regulars. And Bubba Watson, Billy Horschel, Charley Hoffman, and the Tour commissioner, Jay Monahan, formed a riding group—their own peloton—and challenged each other during the rides, urging each other on, pushing and pulling each other along the way.

In May 2020, you might remember that, with the world at a standstill, ESPN aired a documentary about the basketball legend Michael Jordan, called *The Last Dance*. The show was so well done, and millions of people who were otherwise stuck at home tuned into it. It provided a much-needed communal experience in a time of being apart.

I grew up in the 1990s, a decade Jordan dominated. I always wanted Air Jordans, but my dad would go to Payless and get me Shaqs. (That was the immigrant mindset, one I still have.) Jordan is the greatest of all time, aka the G.O.A.T., in my opinion. The documentary on him was inspiring because it was about, in its essence, his greatness—where it came from and how he used his work ethic, focus, preparation, and determination to achieve it. As the documentary showed, it wasn't always a pretty process— Jordan, at times, was cutthroat in his pursuit of excellence. And he demanded a lot from his teammates and coaches, though he never demanded more from them than he did from himself. Jordan was still a work in progress when it came to doing better, for sure, as we all are. But I loved the show and I loved him for his greatness.

That month, as the show was still airing, ESPN called and asked if I would do a Peloton ride with a *Last Dance* theme when it was over, as kind of a celebration. They did not need to ask me twice. I went back and rewatched all of the episodes and designed a playlist based on some of the songs that appeared in the show. It made for a perfect 1990s hip-hop ride, with songs from DMX, Kool Moe Dee, and A Tribe Called Quest. I tried to channel Jordan as I prepared for the ride, with what I call a "Game 6" mentality. That is, I had the mentality that the championship was going to be won now, that there would be no need to pack an outfit for a final Game 7.

The ride took place on May 16, 2020. Some twenty-seven thousand riders joined me in my living room. It was such a dope ride, with amazing feedback from the community, and it was thrilling to give MJ's greatness the proper treatment. It felt like a championship moment. I validated the experience on the spot. I felt like I was on top of the world.

And then, just nine days later, that world came crashing down on top of me and made me realize that my journey to doing better was nowhere near complete, that there were other bigger, more difficult, summits that I needed to climb.

• • •

It is June 2, 2020. I am supposed to be instructing a class in a few days. But for the first time ever, I have decided to cancel it.

It's been less than two weeks—eight days that have felt like a decade—since George Floyd lay helplessly on the pavement and suffocated to death under the knee of a police officer. This was after Breonna Taylor, Ahmaud Arbery, Michael Brown, Eric Garner, Trayvon Martin. . . .

It's been a lifetime.

I'm angry. Scared. Exhausted. There is no other conclusion than the obvious one: In the United States of America, Black lives do not have equal value. Somewhere down deep, I knew this already. The Floyd murder, in the wake of the succession of other killings, has finally brought that realization to the surface for me. I choke on my jumbled emotions. I can't breathe, either.

The class I am supposed to teach is taking place in my apartment. For more than a month now, I have been inviting people into my home. Three times a week, twenty thousand-plus people and me in my living room. "Live from Home" had been a way for me to open up, a way for all of us to come together as one. No longer. We can't be "one" if some of us are still held apart.

I realized something then, something important. Though I had been inviting people into my home, I had not really let them in. Not fully. I still had my guard up. It was always up and always has been. That's the nature of what happens when there is a lifetime of this. It can be difficult for people to understand, especially for those people for whom their guard rarely, if ever, has to be raised in everyday life.

By this point, I had been on the bike and instructing for nearly seven years. And not once had I contemplated canceling a class. As I've said, I viewed every single class as an opportunity—to be great, to help others be great, to bring more people into the community.

And the "Live from Home" classes had felt even more important. Because of the pandemic, there was an urgency to them. We
needed them. I needed them.

But not now. No part of me wanted to instruct a class at this
moment. I didn't feel like getting on the bike. I didn't feel like
motivating anyone else, much less myself. I didn't feel like having
other people in my home with me. I wanted to be here alone. I
wanted to do what I had done so many times during my childhood, when I was depressed or anxious or in pain. I wanted to
curl up on my couch and not move, for anything.

So that's what I did. I curled up on that couch in a daze. I
should have been in the first stages of putting together a playlist
for my class, but my thoughts blocked everything. I looked back
on my life and realized something for the first time: So much of
what I did and didn't do, the choices and decisions I made, had
been driven and shaped by fear—the type of fear that comes hand
in hand with the devaluation of a life.

My dad had sent me to military school, as he said, to buy me
time to figure things out and to keep me from doing the dumb
things that might land me in jail. But behind those reasons, I
realized now, was something else, something more significant.
It was fear. He had sent me to military school, really, to keep
me alive. I had been getting into trouble, and the trouble had
been escalating. Who knew how far I would take it? My dad was
aware, somewhere deep down, that I might be on the verge of
making the type of mistake—something big or even something
small—that could very well be my last.

I thought about that lady in our neighborhood, the one who

used to call the cops on me, even years after we had moved in, how her act felt scary and demeaning at the time, how the possibility that she might call the cops was *always* in the back of my mind, even as I walked the streets of *my* neighborhood. Our town cops, to their credit, eventually stopped taking her calls seriously and would just drive by and give me a wave, but that didn't change how I felt about it.

I realized now that my mom asked me to take off my du-rag whenever I left the house because of that neighbor and people like her. I realized now that my dad used to demand that I turn down my car radio when I got near her house, and that he told me not to slam the car door or let the dogs bark, all because of her. He was fearful—and so was my mom and so was I—of making her feel uncomfortable. What we never really stopped to consider was our own comfort.

I realized now, too, that my mom's and dad's insistence on always being well-dressed and well-presented was also, at least partially, predicated on fear. They were fearful of being looked down upon, or looked at as an "other." Our fear had confined us to a box. And it wasn't just our neighbor who confined us to this box. It was society. My neighbor was just a representative of the greater whole.

I thought about the fact that, to this day, I still text my mom when I get back home from going out, just to ease her mind, just so she knows I am safe. She realizes that anything can happen to me from Point A to Point B. She feels fear.

I thought about how every time I drive somewhere, I have to maintain my discipline over distractions. I have been pulled over way more than a dozen times in my life. Always for one reason, and one reason alone, which I bet you can guess. I was pulled over so many times when I lived in Brooklyn, in fact, that a security guard at Peloton gave me a Police Benevolent Association membership card so that I could show it to the officer as he approached my car on the side of the road. The idea was that maybe the card would convince the cop to let me go without further interaction. Most of the cops who pulled me over, even when I had that card, did not do that. In fact, they tended to double down on the humiliation. One night in Brooklyn I was pulled over because I supposedly looked like a drug dealer. Another cop who pulled me over pulled a gun on me.

I could have easily been distracted in those moments and not maintained my discipline and yelled, "Yo, what the fuck?" I could have let my emotions take hold of me. And if the cop who had pulled me over had been going through a bad day, or had an ego, or whatever, there's a chance I might not have made it home that day, and my mom never would have received a text.

The thing about this fear is that it's not just within me. It's within *we*. And we are far worse off as a society because of it.

As I thought through all of this on the couch, I realized that I was sick and tired of being afraid, and that I needed to do something about it. What I needed to do was to help other people understand that fear, in the hopes that, maybe, they could help re-create a society where it no longer existed. I wasn't the president or anything like that. I couldn't go on national TV and address the nation. But I *could* reach some people. I had a platform, but up to this point, I had been reluctant to use it in this manner. No more, I decided. I knew that this potentially had consequences, for me and for my career. I knew I could anger or alienate a good number of my riders, most of whom were white. But it was a risk I now knew I had to take.

So I decided to do the class.

It was not going to be an ordinary class, however.

I first called Robin. I told her what and how I was feeling.

"I don't speak much about public issues," I told her. "That's not been my lane."

Robin just listened.

"But I am going to speak now in my class. It's time to break through the barrier."

When I was done talking, Robin said, simply: "AT, you were hired here to be yourself. Do what you're going to do."

I hung up and called Shakah, my producer.

"The class is on," I said.

But I had to do something else first.

• • •

That night, I thought about my mom's directive to me as a kid, about how I should hang out with as many different types of people as possible. Because I had indeed lived out her dictum, I had become conscious that the big labels we put on groups of people (white, Black, Hispanic, Asian) fail, in a lot of ways, to recognize the often significant differences of the subsets within those groups.

My own background is a good example. Black people are not the monolith that some presume us to be. My experience and background as a second-generation Black Haitian immigrant is different in some very significant ways from the experience and background of my friend Archie, who is a second-generation Black Nigerian immigrant, and is also different in some very significant ways from the experience and background of an African American. I wondered if the broad, sweeping labels we put on groups of people did more harm than help in the end.

But I was also aware that none of these differences were recognized within the greater society and wouldn't likely be anytime soon. That's the way it was, and I knew I had to come to terms with that. I knew that to the greater, mostly white, world, I was Black, period. And I knew that with that, there came some serious responsibility on my part.

I had been one of the few Black instructors at Flywheel. I was the first Black instructor at Peloton.

These "firsts" meant something to me. I felt the responsibility to work extra hard and "make it" and do it all flawlessly because I knew I represented something more than just me. But what I hadn't realized at the time of those "firsts" was that my responsibility went much deeper than just working hard and trying to be flawless. I had missed something. On the bike, I shared *my* life and *my* pain and *my* motivation. But I had not shared the lives and pain and motivation of people who look like me.

And I'd had the platform to do all of this, right there in front of me. It shocked me when I realized this. I had the opportunity to do something, to help right a wrong. I had been helping people, for sure. I had reached a summit of do better. But there was more that I could do. Much more. There were other summits that I had yet to climb. And I hadn't seen them. My awareness, I realized, had not been at a full 360 degrees. I had failed to check my blind spots. So much of doing better is about having that awareness, that empathy, that ability to at least try to put ourselves in the shoes of others. I'd had the opportunity to do that, and I had failed at it. It's not that I left people who looked like me behind on purpose. It wasn't willful. It was just that I had not fully thought it through. There was an entire part of doing better that I had neglected. I had stood on the summit, and I had not seen a large group of people who needed my help.

I'd been accepted by all groups of people. I had followed my mom's orders. In high school, I'd go to an all-white party in East Hampton. The door would open. They'd let me in, no problem, but would eye my homies with weird suspicion.

I said "yes, ma'am" and "yes, sir" when speaking to my elders. This practice went back to my Haitian parents and the level of respect they expected me to show them and the rest of the world. That created an aura around me as a "nice guy." I smiled a lot. That helped me, too. I wore nice clothes. Some of my friends teasingly called me "white." That's the way society works.

I had fit in. I had been accepted. But being the "token," or being labeled as such, was a horrible thing. What it meant was that I had been accepted but that others like me—the people for whom I had responsibility—had not. And they were suffering because of it. Their lives mattered less because of this lack of understanding. I realized that I had not been doing the job that I signed up for internally. I had, instead, been focused on me and not we.

For many riders at Peloton, I was the first, and maybe only, Black person whom they had invited into their homes, their lives. It took me a few rides to realize this, and when I did realize it, it shocked me. I had expressed myself unapologetically. Peloton—the company, the riders—had accepted me for who I was, embraced me.

But they seemed to view other Black people as just a demographic, which blunted their ability to see them as actual individual human beings. My riders saw me as a human being. But others were not being treated the same way.

I faced some uncomfortable questions. How had I not communicated to my riders that I was like people who looked like me and they were like me? How had I not communicated to them that I, too, had been pulled over in my car multiple times just because of the color of my skin? How had I not communicated to them how humiliating and scary that was?

I decided that it was time for me to confront all of this. I had a responsibility, to other minorities and especially to young Black men. That responsibility was to try to open the door so that my riders could see other people the same way they saw me. To do better.

• • •

The day after I made the decision to not cancel my ride, I decided to take another step. I had, the day before, posted a black square on my Instagram page, part of Blackout Tuesday, a movement that millions took part in across the globe, supposedly to protest racism and police brutality.

Now, a day later, that gesture just felt hollow. It felt like an easy, unthinking way out. Signaling virtue means nothing. It is not *practicing* virtue.

I hated that I had participated in it without forethought. I left the post up but decided to take a big step forward. ***Less caption, more action*** was what was needed.

This phrase, in a simple sense, is about how we should put our social media use in context. Maybe the biggest problem with social media is the way it disembodies us physically, mentally, and emotionally. Everything we say on social media, just as everything we say in real life, should have real meaning behind it. Proper use of it means treating ourselves and everyone else on social media as if we were actually physically present with each other. We need to treat everyone—including ourselves—with respect, empathy, and love.

But the implications of this phrase are much bigger than just social media. It's never enough to just "say" something in life, no matter where you say it. Actions are what count. Posting a blacked-out square on Instagram might be a nice gesture and a show of solidarity and might make the poster feel like he or she has done something, but nothing of importance has been accomplished if there is no action to back it up. "Less caption, more action" starts with believing in ourselves and standing firm in those beliefs. It means speaking up for what's right, but not stopping there. Putting action—and not just captions—into those beliefs is what matters most.

For me in that moment, it meant that it was time to put myself out there, something that "nice" Alex had never really done. It was time for more action. I would follow through on that myself from then on. I would continue to do my job as best I could, to hustle, to represent in that way. But I would also start to be more myself. I would wear a du-rag to corporate meetings, wear sweats to work. I wanted people to see it was still me. They liked me, I knew. I wanted them to see that they shouldn't judge people like me so fast. My mom used to dress a certain way to fit into greater society. I dressed a certain way in the hopes that others would fit into greater society.

I propped my phone up on a table and pushed "record." It was a beautiful early summer day, the sun flooding my apartment. I wore a black du-rag and a gray hoodie with PHENOMENALLY BLACK written on the front of it. I felt angry, and I didn't try to hide it. I didn't wear the smile I usually do. I wanted people to see me, to see the rawness and the emotion. I wanted them to deal, face-to-face, with the "Angry Black Guy," and push them to ask themselves why the Angry Black Guy always seems so damn angry.

I started talking into the camera.

"I've been searching for the right words to come up here and speak with y'all. But there are no right words to describe what I'm feeling right now."

I cut to the chase quickly.

"I need y'all to wake the hell up. My people are dying. Black individuals like myself, young Black men, kings and queens, are not making it home safely. They get killed in broad daylight on camera. This has got to stop, man."

I continued.

"Some of y'all think this racism shit isn't even real. Listen . . . racism is real. Racism is in your life. I'm in your life. I'm not exempt from it 'cause I work at Peloton where I got cameras in my face when y'all show me love. . . . My life is not a trend. Our lives are not trends. My life is more than a fucking hashtag. . . . I need you to really wake up. I need you to ultimately do better. . . . It's time to evolve."

I stopped the recording and posted the video on my Instagram page. It was the rawest thing I'd ever done in public. Four minutes and twenty-seven seconds of it. I still felt raw, though. Still angry. Still scared.

A lot of the time when a Black person speaks, many people turn the other way and don't even show up for the conversation. They shy away because of the truths and the difficulty of those truths. Those truths and that difficulty make them feel uncomfortable. I knew that people could click on my Instagram post, see what it was about, and then quickly click off if they wanted to.

But there was another place I had to take that message to where people would be less likely to turn away, a place where we already felt comfortable together, an audience that was already there, waiting and seated on a stationary bike, ready to be moved.

• • •

The next day—June 5, 2020—at 9:30 A.M., Dave took his place behind the camera, the red light came on, and I started pedaling.

"One-two! One-Two!" I said, in something a little less than a yell. A military school vibe.

My energy was so different, unlike any other ride I'd ever done. I tried to force a smile as I said hello to the class through the camera, but it didn't come. I was raw as hell, emotional and angry. I focused on keeping those emotions in check as much as I could. I didn't want to lose control of the class. I didn't want it to be about me, individually. I wanted to reach people. I wanted them to really *listen* to my words.

"It's going to get uncomfortable. It's going to get tough," I said. "But, dammit, life is uncomfortable."

I'd chosen my playlist with care. Every song had a point—the same point. I played T.I.'s "New National Anthem," with its haunting chorus about the Black experience in America:

"Home of the brave and the free . . . / Free just to murder me."

I hit the class with Lil Wayne's "Shoot Me Down." His refrain, too, told the story:

"Please don't shoot me down 'cause I'm flyin'."

The music set the tone and the mood. I filled up the rest of the space with my words.

"It's not about me, it's about we. How we treat each other, how we ride together, shine together. . . . For some of y'all, I'm the only African American in your household. Others are like me, others who provide light to the world . . . others who walk like me, talk like me, but don't have the opportunity that I have."

I worked my riders hard in that class. Hill followed by interval followed by hill, trying to connect the physical and the mental. It was as much for me as it was for them. Toward the end of the ride, I made a direct plea to the people taking the class, both the ones who were there live, and the ones who would see it later on the recording. They had all accepted me. It was part of the pattern. I had always been accepted. But it made me feel like shit that they hadn't accepted my people, my culture. Acceptance is the key, and it takes effort, an effort to see beyond one's own horizons. A lot of people think just because they aren't racist—just because they were comfortable with me and had allowed me into their homes—that they are not part of the problem. But they are if they aren't proactive about it, if they don't work on the empathy and the sympathy and their awareness and their curiosity, if they sit it all out on the sidelines, if they don't teach their children and talk to their friends about true equality and the value of all lives.

"Try to find the capacity in your heart to change," I said.

I signed off. The camera light went out.

I looked at Dave as a wave of exhaustion hit me. He stood there for a second and then said, in a quiet voice, "You went there, man." He put his hand on my shoulder. It felt like he was holding me up.

The feedback I got from my actions during those two days was immediate. The overwhelming reaction was positive and affirming, to both the Instagram post and the Peloton class. There were some people, however, who did not like what I did, and they made some noise about it. John, Peloton's CEO, received a handful of letters from my riders. Some complained that this type of activism was not what they had signed up for with Peloton. Others went further than that, telling John that they quit Peloton, that I was the worst thing that had ever happened to the company, and that I should be fired.

People like that—who weren't receptive to the message at all, and were, in fact, turned off by it—are a big part of the general problem, of course. But the fact that they took the time to write John made me feel that all was not lost on them and that, in fact, maybe even some progress had been made. They might not have been receptive to the message, but for them to take the step and the time to write in meant that they at least heard some of what I had to say. They had been forced to confront an uncomfortable feeling. It was a step.

John, to his credit, did not cower or back down. In fact, he doubled down on the issue and amplified it. The company started a speaker series featuring some of my fellow instructors that focused on racial issues (there were, by this time, a good number of people of color who were instructors at Peloton). When asked by the *New York Times* if what I had done violated Peloton's rules against political activism by instructors, the company responded that, in this case, it was not a political issue, it was a human rights one. And, later that same month, John announced that Peloton was giving $100 million over the next four years to fight racial injustice and inequity. Among the programs funded by that money: a $500,000 donation to the NAACP Legal Defense and Education Fund, a partnership with Beyoncé to help students in need attend historically Black colleges, and the donation of Peloton equipment and app subscriptions to communities of need.

My actions did come with a cost, though. The aura I had created in my first four-plus years at Peloton was now different. It went from "everybody loves AT!" to, well, "not *everyone* loves AT."

I was cool with that.

• • •

I want to make this clear before I go any further: Our country has made a lot of progress since its founding. I love the United States of America and its promise. The arc of its progress—just like the arc of our own individual progress—is not always a straight upward line. It can be circuitous. But I believe that, by our very nature as Americans, we strive to keep it moving up. The promise of that progress is a big reason why both of my parents came here in the first place. It is part of the American Dream.

We are a vast country with multitudes of different people. Those differences—and how we are able to coexist and even prosper because of them—are our superpower, which is something we seem to have forgotten in recent years. We need to remember it again.

But we also have much in common with each other, much more than not. We share this country and its promise and progress. That commonality is important. We all have greatness within us. We have all had to overcome some negativity in our lives. We have all felt like outsiders at some time or another. The story of America is one of overcoming negativity and activating our greatness, and of people who felt like outsiders coming together to progress as one. This is our promise.

Having said all of that, there is still much work to be done. And our progress, our freedoms, are not "free." They require work and vigilance. They require that we confront some uncomfortable truths. They require us to do better.

America, as a country, is working its way up the mountain to the summit. It's up to us to help make sure it gets there.

• • •

This time in my life completely changed me and my career, for the better. It made me more cognizant of the world around me.

It made me more empathetic. It made me more fully understand what doing better was all about.

It really drove the point home for me that do better isn't just one summit. It isn't a static entity. It changes. It evolves. Every summit we reach is an opportunity to progress even more in attaining new ones.

The experience also made me think about my peloton, of friends, family, and the stories of others. One of those stories, in particular, came to mind. It's the story of someone who I think went through a transformation similar to mine. It's the story of LeBron James.

LeBron is, of course, one of the best players in basketball history. You already know that I believe the "best-ever" title belongs to Jordan. But LeBron isn't too far behind and is, in my book, the best all-around player the game has ever seen.

LeBron, like Jay-Z, grew up under difficult circumstances—his father was never around, and he grew up in the poverty-stricken sections of Akron, Ohio. But he found basketball, worked his ass off on his game, and jumped to the NBA straight from high school. There, he was an immediate star, but he never took his eye off of the end goal. "I only want to make my teammates better" was his most common refrain. Twenty years later, he still does the same thing.

Twenty years later, too, he still outworks everyone in the gym at practice. This is the little secret of the greats. Yes, they have natural, God-given talent. But they maximize that talent with their work and their habits, and it becomes muscle memory. "Your life is what you make it. It's how you approach every day and how you spend that twenty-four-hour block," he once said, a quote that has stuck with me.

LeBron has gone on to win four NBA Championships, four NBA MVP awards, and two Olympic gold medals. He's the NBA's all time leading scorer. But most impressive—and inspirational—to me is what he's done off the court, with his platform.

Like Jay-Z, LeBron has a foundation. His focuses primarily on providing educational opportunities for underprivileged kids and families in his hometown of Akron. (He built an elementary school there that he funds himself with an annual $1 million donation.) His foundation grants around $5 million a year and has attracted substantial donations from people such as the rapper Drake. Like Jay-Z, LeBron focused on trying to ensure that others didn't have to go through what he did as a child. His work has positively altered the lives of thousands of children and families.

In addition to that, LeBron has done even more good. He has become a powerful voice for the powerless. LeBron and his Miami Heat teammates donned hoodies in memory of Trayvon Martin before a game to raise awareness of the killing, a symbolic gesture that resonated around the country.

Two years later, LeBron wore an I CAN'T BREATHE T-shirt after Eric Garner was killed (those were Garner's last words). LeBron spoke up for voting rights during the 2016 and 2020 presidential elections. He wore another I CAN'T BREATHE T-shirt and spoke out extensively after the murder of George Floyd.

We're all fortunate that LeBron has used his platform to speak up. What's unfortunate is the number of times he has had to do so. Jordan may be the G.O.A.T. on the court. But LeBron is the G.O.A.T. off of it.

LeBron has done all of this against some very strong headwinds. A prominent news commentator once told him to "shut up and dribble." A U.S. president spoke out against him on social media and, at some of his rallies, led a "LeBron James sucks" chant. LeBron has had his house vandalized with racist graffiti.

And yet, he continues to speak out. Just shutting up and dribbling is not morally viable anymore. And neither, I decided, was just shutting up and pedaling.

When I got to Peloton, I told myself that I wanted to be the LeBron James of the spin class game. What I meant back then was that I wanted to be great at it. I still want to be the LeBron James of the spin class game, but what I mean now is that I want to be great on the bike *and* off of it.

LeBron taught me that whatever you do in life—if you're a lawyer, teacher, grocery bagger—don't wait until your career is over to use your platform. Do it in real time. We all have a platform. No matter what we do in life, we can help those around us, our community. And whatever we do off our "court" amplifies what we do on it. When provided a platform, we are given a great responsibility: *to do better.*

CHAPTER 15

VALIDATION

We've talked about the concept of validation already, but I want to drill down a bit more here, since it is among the most important things we can do to activate our greatness. There are two types of validation—one that we receive from the outside (promotions at work would be an example) and one that comes from within us. The second one is far more important than the first. That one is actualized when we stop waiting for other people out there to tell us we're doing a good job, that we're on the right track. It's when we realize that it's all about how *we* feel about and view ourselves. It comes when we stop suppressing the positive things in our lives, when we *know* we are worthy. We are doing the work. We have value. We are great. When we do this, we start to operate on a totally different frequency. We radiate. We feel good, look good, and are able to do better. And guess what? When we validate ourselves from within, the outside validation will come naturally.

. . .

On October 21, 2021, I traveled out to East Hampton for the day. Because of COVID and work, I hadn't been out there in a while. It had been too long since I'd visited.

It was a perfect autumn day, the kind of day the Hamptons—with their wide vistas of golden fields that meet an endless blue ocean—seem designed for. I went to the public beach where I used to swim and hang out with friends. I went to my favorite Italian deli and had lunch.

I drove around town, past my old schools. I touched base with some of my old friends. I met my former kindergarten teacher, Susan Verde, at a coffee shop, and gave her a big hug and we talked about elementary school and what she'd been up to. I stopped by to see Jerome, his mom, and his niece, who is my goddaughter. Jerome still lived in the same blue house. At one point during my visit, I went upstairs to Jerome's old room and gazed down at the floor where I had spent more nights than I could count.

Near the end of the day, as the sun began to set and the air began to chill, I went back to the neighborhood where I grew up. I parked the car in front of my old house (which my parents had left some years before) and looked up at the front door, the same door I had avoided walking into so many times.

I walked down to the path that led to the water, that place of solace for me when I was younger, the same place where, not even a decade before, I had contemplated a world without me. It looked pretty much unchanged—same trees, same patch of cattails. When I emerged from the path, I stood and looked out over Three Mile Harbor, and something just hit me. I started to cry—to bawl, really—as I had done so often in this very spot. This time, though, it was for different reasons.

. . .

Let me back up just a bit. After the George Floyd episode and as I continued to progress at Peloton, I started to think more about my future, about business opportunities, and about how I could give back to the community in ways that transcended the bike. I've always said that if I died today and people only knew me for riding a bike that went nowhere, I would have failed at life and failed to take full advantage of the opportunities that had opened up for me. I wanted to use my platform to take my life to a whole new trajectory, to feed my family, stay inspired, and inspire others along the way, much like Jay-Z and LeBron had done. I wanted to live the most authentic life possible, so that no day ever felt like work. And I wanted to do all of this with the right people.

A few years into my career at Peloton, some brands began to reach out to me, looking for partnerships. I was told by just about everyone that I needed to hire a professional management team, one of the bigwig three-letter agencies in New York or Los Angeles, to represent me. I looked into it and had some meetings and some calls. But I never felt totally comfortable with the vibe I got—these were professional folks with no connection to me who just seemed to be all about maximizing the money. They were great at what they did, no doubt. Their track records spoke for themselves. But I decided that I wanted to do it differently.

The conventional wisdom is that we should never mix friends and business, that doing so clouds judgment and leads to bad endings, for both the friendships and the business. I didn't believe that this was true. My peloton in life is comprised of people who I want to help and see succeed, and who want to help me and see me succeed, of people who know me and understand me and where I came from, and understand my vision and where I want to take things. My business life was part of my life. It seemed to me that it should be approached in the same way.

Both Jay-Z and LeBron have found much success in having their friends involved in their business lives (yet another example of taking an idea or experience from someone we respect but may not personally know and applying it to our own lives). So I decided to do the same. Dave, with his law degree, and Archie, with his experience in start-ups, complemented each other, and me, very well. Together, we would handle endorsements, the growing of the brand, and the philanthropic efforts.

I can't even begin to fully express how important Archie and Dave are to me, and how gratifying it has been to work together with them, as a team. It felt like we were just kids when we started in Brooklyn, with just an idea. We hung out all the time. We had fun together. The transformation of that idea into a reality was such a cool ride. We hung in there during the lows and we validated the highs. We continue to serve as each other's motivation, and when that runs low—as it will, at times—we serve as each other's discipline. Archie and Dave are my business managers. They are my best friends. We have a shared vision, and we execute it with intention. They are an integral part of my business, but more important, they are an integral part of my life.

One of the most important steps we took was starting the Do Better Foundation, which focuses on democratizing wellness. The foundation is a huge part of what we do. It gave everything else we did a purpose.

And in early 2020, they started the process of building a brand. They recruited a friend to create a logo, which would come in handy for later endorsement deals. They started a website and launched an e-shop. Along with every purchase from the shop, we sent out a postcard with the Do Better Pledge, which read:

Dear Fam,

If you're reading this, it means you have chosen to Do Better. That means you've chosen empathy over ignorance, courage over fear, and love over hate. Do Better is not only a mindset, it's also a lifestyle.

I'm letting you know off top it ain't gon' be easy, but I'm counting on YOU to lead with love and execute with intention.

I'm counting on YOU to Do Better.

Much Love,
Alex Toussaint

As we sifted through endorsement offers we kept one thing in mind: Whomever we worked with, in any capacity, had to share our vision of mental, physical, and spiritual health, and of doing better in the community. A brand is about authenticity, first and foremost. People see right through anything false or made up or exaggerated. You be you, be aligned with yourself, and the community will come. A brand is not a social media post ("less caption, more action"). It's something that's created, grown, and nurtured based on something real.

Our first deal was with Ladder, a sports nutrition company that happened to be founded by LeBron James, a deal that made sense, since I was an athlete focused on wellness. We next signed on with Hyperice, a company that focuses on taking care of the body, using ice, heat, percussion, and vibration, to help us both get ready for a workout and recover from one. I liked the people and the company immediately. Hyperice's mission statement—"to help everyone on Earth move better, live better and be better"— had a familiar ring to it and aligned perfectly with our mission.

For all of my life, I had been a Nike guy. Jordan, Kobe, and LeBron—three of Nike's biggest endorsers—had always been my heroes. I had craved fresh Nike high-tops as a kid and had started to wear them all the time when I could finally afford them. I wore Nike apparel when I was on the bike, instructing.

The company noticed. Sometime in 2018, they reached out to us to talk about an endorsement deal. When they first contacted us, I felt like I'd gone to heaven. This was the deal I had dreamed about as a kid.

We went back and forth with them for what turned out to be three years. Something about it never felt exactly right. They seemed to want to partner with us, but they also seemed to be a bit lukewarm about the whole thing. When negotiations began, they kept tweaking the language of the deal in a way that reflected their vision and not ours. It all dragged on. Intuition is something I had begun to really rely on. I believe that it grows in power as we grow, that as we work hard on ourselves, begin to rely on ourselves, and begin to do better by others, we develop that intuition. It makes us feel calm and comfortable when there's uncertainty and able to be levelheaded when it comes to making decisions.

In the meantime, we started looking at other companies. Jay-Z, at the time, had recently been named creative director at Puma Basketball. His imprint was all over the brand. Dave contacted the vice president of marketing at Puma. She messaged him back and expressed interest When we spoke with them, they listened to our ideas and supported the vision. From a business sense, they were trying to make a splash in the fitness sector of their global brand. It seemed like a good fit. Like Peloton, they were interested in letting me be me. This is hugely important when it comes to any partnerships we have in life—business or personal.

In late 2021, Nike finally offered us a contract in writing. By this point, I sort of realized that it probably wasn't going to work with them, but I wanted to get the actual contract in hand anyway, as a way of recognizing what we had accomplished.

In the end, we moved forward with Puma. In the deal, Puma agreed to produce cobranded products, including my own capsule collection for both men's and women's wear. We came up with the idea of a signature biking shoe, and they loved it. It is the first signature cycling shoe since Lance Armstrong had one, and the first-ever signature shoe from an athlete in the fitness industry.

Puma even agreed to help with the Do Better Foundation, with money, product, and publicity.

It so happened that Puma publicly announced the deal on that same October day when I was in the Hamptons, just before I walked down the path to the water, which made that moment even more extraordinary, jubilant, poignant, emotional—a crazy mix.

But let me be clear about something: The Puma deal was not validation. These types of outside, material things are not validating. I believed in what I was doing. That deal merely meant that someone else saw it, too. I really believe that once you have real self-validation, other people will see it and recognize it, just as they see our inner lights shining through. That's how we have to view these things—as someone else seeing something in you that you already knew was there. Viewing it this way helps us keep it real and keep it in check and keep the focus where it should be.

• • •

That same year, I bought my first house. It was out in New Jersey, not too far away from the Peloton studios, but far enough out of the city that I could have an actual lawn. My goal was to make it like Jerome's place in East Hampton—not just a house, but a home.

Initially, I had envisioned buying the East Hampton house I grew up in. It seemed to me to be some sort of destiny, like it would bring my story all the way around, full circle. But the more I thought about it, the more I realized that if I really wanted a "home," I would also need a clean slate. That house in East Hampton had too many demons lurking within it, too many reminders of the terrible state I had been in when I lived there. I didn't need that pain to get motivated anymore. I'd moved past it. I was motivated by my vision for the future now, for taking this all as far as it could go and taking along as many people as I could with me.

My new house would become the home I had always wanted, filled with love, devoid of negativity. I had a room that I designated for my mom, where she could visit and be comfortable and eventually move into when and if she wanted to do so. I had space for my brothers when they wanted to visit. I even had space for my dad, too. It was a family place.

A few months after I bought and moved into the new house, I called my mom.

"Mom, you can retire now," I told her.

My mom was a tireless worker and had been all of her life. She always said that she would never retire because she'd never want to. But I'd been keeping an eye on her. She still loved her job and still loved the kids and her coworkers but, after almost fifty years of working and studying and commuting, she deserved some rest. This, in the end, was the reason I had joined Peloton and did what I did. I didn't really care about the fame and the accolades. I just wanted to honor her, to recognize all of what she had done for me—the commuting, the work, the parenting, her dedication. And I was finally able to do that for her. It was a way for me to validate all of the sacrifices she had made for me in her life. She didn't need that validation. But she deserved it. It was one of the most gratifying moments of my life.

About a month before her official retirement, she came out

to New Jersey to visit me. She had a different vibe about her, like she was relaxed but excited for what lay ahead of her. During the visit, I showed her my car. She got a twinkle in her eye and asked me for the keys. I handed them over, a little uncertain about what she was going to do. She had a huge, mischievous smile on her face as she hopped in. She started the engine and peeled out of the driveway and then raced around the neighborhood.

She was going to enjoy retirement.

CHAPTER 16

COOLDOWN

At the end of every one of my classes, we do a few minutes of cooling down. This part of the ride might seem like an easy thing to skip . . . after all, we just worked hard and we're only a few moments away from logging off. So why not move on to our next task of the day? But taking some time to cool down is vitally important to do, in the class and in life. We need to recover from the rigors of the work we've done, to process and contextualize it and, importantly, to validate it all. There's no need to rush.

But realize this: Cooling down doesn't mean we're shutting off completely. It's merely a transitory period, a necessary recharge where we align our physical, emotional, and mental selves. That way we can stay ready and relentless in the pursuit of doing better and remain in peak condition to stay focused on all of the self-motivation that is required to get there. We've moved with a purpose. Now we get to execute with intention

. . .

As, hopefully, the worst of the pandemic finally passed, I pushed myself even harder on and off the bike. We were back in the studio then. I looked at every class as an opportunity to help us all process two years of grief, fear, and loneliness. We needed to validate the fact that we had made it through. And we owed something to the people who hadn't: To grab our opportunities in life, every single day. To feel good, look good, and do better. To overcome the negativity in our lives. To activate our greatness.

The work of the Do Better Foundation ramped up. Among the highlights was a trip I made down to Joint Base Andrews. The military always held a special place for me, and I knew that a lot of military folks had been having a hard time with their mental health and didn't always have the resources in place that they needed to deal with it. On my visit, I did a talk for the aircrew, with Chief Kaleth Wright, the master chief of the air force. I donated some Peloton bikes and subscriptions to the app to the base, in order to help the aircrew with their mental and physical health. I dedicated the gift in the name of my uncle, Ronald Toussaint, the air force master sergeant who had served on Air Force One.

My goal with the foundation and, really, everything I do from here on out is to do what my mom did for me: Provide others with opportunities, and especially immigrants from Haiti. To provide opportunities for education, for picking themselves up. The opportunity to activate their greatness.

As the pandemic restrictions lifted, I started to go to NBA basketball games again. I had missed watching the games in person. I still played basketball weekly, as part of my therapeutic regimen. And I still harbored dreams of glory on the court.

My high school playing career had been fun, but I'd always been a role player on those teams, mainly because I had never fully committed to the game. That had left a void within me, one I wanted to fill. I knew I'd never make the NBA, but I wondered if there were other outlets. When I started to get a little traction as a spin instructor, I started to dream a bit more. And I wrote down a goal: One day, I wanted to play in the NBA All-Star Celebrity Game.

One night in the early part of 2022, I was courtside for a New York Knicks game at Madison Square Garden when a man approached me. He introduced himself and said he worked for the NBA.

"Do you play basketball? Are you any good?"

In that moment, I was not going to say no to either of those questions.

"Well, then, how would you like to play in the celebrity game this year?"

I wasn't going to say no to that question, either.

In all of those years of playing basketball weekly, I realized that I had been preparing for something that, until that moment, was just a dream. It made me think of a phrase I say to my classes all the time: *When you stay ready, you never have to get ready*.

What this means, simply put, is to get obsessed about your passions and your craft, yourself, and others. Build—and use— all of those mental muscles we talked about earlier so that when an opportunity presents itself, you'll be ready for it.

I did two things before I went to Cleveland for the game: I mapped out a speech for after the game, and I booked a private jet home. I did these two things because I planned on winning the game's MVP. I wanted to be ready with something to say when I won it, and I didn't want to have to take the trophy through airport security to get it home. This wasn't cockiness on my part. It was a mindset. A belief.

The game featured a rather random mix of celebrities. The artist Machine Gun Kelly. The comedian Tiffany Haddish. The NFL star Myles Garrett. Gianmarco Tamberi, an Olympic gold medal–winning high jumper. A female member of the Harlem Globetrotters. The mayor of Cleveland.

Before the game, I did not feel nervous. I felt exactly how I do before I get on the bike for class: excited to show the world what I can do.

The game was so fun. I played hard. I dribbled the point. I dished out assists. I scored eighteen points and had six rebounds and five assists. And I was, indeed, named the game's MVP.

As I stood on the court holding the trophy and doing interviews with the media, I realized that the actual winning of the trophy wasn't what really mattered in this case. What mattered was what I had overcome to get to this moment—the negativity, the backtracking, all of those head-down moments in my life. I held my head high now. What mattered was the belief I had in myself. What mattered was all of the work I had put in, all of the things I had done—invisible to most others—to get to that day. *I had rewritten my own narrative.* Winning the trophy was just validation of all of that.

As the last of my interviews wound down on the court, I felt my phone vibrate in my pocket. I grabbed it to see who was calling. It was my dad, the same man who had never come to see any of my games when I was a kid, the same man who I had hated for much of my life but had now come to understand more completely and even genuinely love. He had been watching the game on TV, from start to finish.

"Congratulations, son," he said. I could hear his smile through the phone. I could see my own smile reflected in the trophy.

And I realized then that though there would be many more mountains to climb in the future, the two of us were nearing a summit of one right now. And in that moment, we had locked arms, helping each other get there.

. . .

Like I said at the very beginning of this book, I don't think my story is any more important than anyone else's—there are so many people out there who have had extreme challenges they've had to overcome. But I do hope that this story is instructive, that it can help. I truly believe that no matter what you brought to this book—the need for inspiration, motivation, a different outlook on life—you have it in your power to do what I did, to move from a place of supreme negativity to a place of teamwork, light, and love.

You know why?

Because there is only one you. And I *see* you. Whether you showed up as a volunteer at a food bank handing out a turkey or showed up as the person being handed that turkey, you are a work in progress. We all are.

So work toward that progress. Concentrate on making your way up that mountain. Keep moving. Keep pushing. Feel good. Look good.

When you reach that summit—*because you will!*—do better. Lend a hand and bring someone else up with you. And then come back down and do it all over again with someone else.

Remember, it's the little things that matter. Fall in love with the journey. Embrace that destination.

We can all get there if we remember—and do—these things.

I can't wait to see you along the way.

ACKNOWLEDGMENTS

First off, I want to thank God, because without Him, none of this is possible.

I want to thank my parents for their hard work, sacrifice, vision, mindset, and understanding, and for all they have done for my brothers and me. I love you more than anything and I hope I'm making you proud.

I want to thank Archie and Dave, my partners in business and in life. We're just getting started.

I want to thank my agent, Richard Pine, and my editors, Amy Einhorn and Shannon Criss, and all of the great people at Henry Holt for helping to make this project come to life and expertly seeing it through to the end.

I also want to thank myself . . . for never fucking quitting.

ABOUT THE AUTHOR

ALEX TOUSSAINT is a Peloton instructor and Puma athlete. A hybrid of high-performance athlete and motivational coach, Toussaint is a titan within the fitness community and is widely respected for his authenticity and positivity. He thrives at the intersection of fitness, tech, music, sports, fashion, entertainment, and community. In 2020, he founded the Do Better Foundation, whose mission is to promote and provide broader access to wellness services and resources.